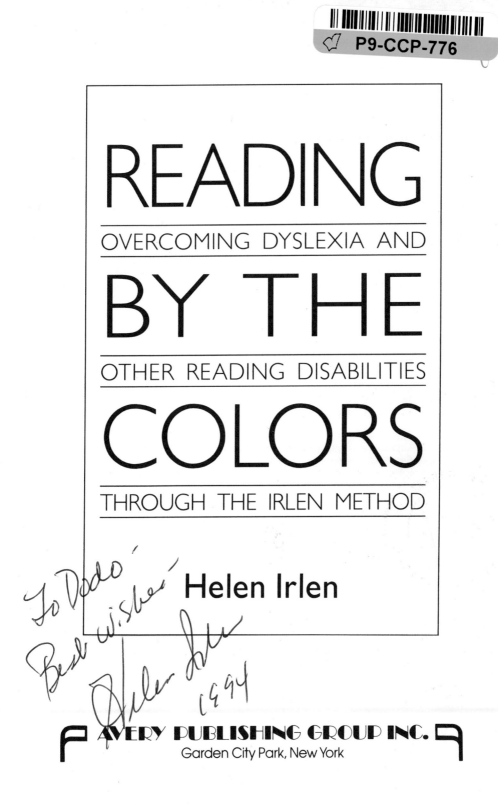

READING

OVERCOMING DYSLEXIA AND

BY THE

OTHER READING DISABILITIES

COLORS

THROUGH THE IRLEN METHOD

Helen Irlen

To Dodo~
Best Wishes~
Helen Irlen
1994

AVERY PUBLISHING GROUP INC.
Garden City Park, New York

Cover Design: Rudy Shur and Janine Eisner-Wall
In-House Editor: Arthur Vidro
Typesetting: Coghill Book Typesetting Co., Richmond, Virginia

The following are reprinted with permission of the copyright owner, Perceptual Development Corp., for which acknowledgment is here made: the washout effect (page 36), the halo effect (page 38), the rivers effect (page 40), the swirl effect (page 42), the shaky effect (page 44), the blurry effect (page 45), the seesaw effect (page 46), and the cube exercise (page 140).

Library of Congress Cataloging-in-Publication Data

Irlen, Helen, 1945-
    Reading by the colors : overcoming dyslexia and other reading
  disabilities through the Irlen method / Helen Irlen.
        p.   cm.
    Includes index.
    ISBN 0-89529-476-1 (hardback) — ISBN 0-89529-482-6 (pbk.)
    1. Dyslexia. 2. Color vision.   I. Title.
    [DNLM: 1. Color Perception. 2. Dyslexia—rehabilitation.
  3. Vision Disorders—rehabilitation.   WL 340 I69r]
  RC394.W6I75 1991
  616.85'53—dc20
  DNLM/DLC
  for Library of Congress   91-17212
                                                    CIP

Printed in the United States of America

10 9 8 7 6 5 4 3 2

Contents

Acknowledgments   v

Foreword   ix

1. Why This Book?   1
2. Discovery   9
3. What is Scotopic Sensitivity Syndrome?   29
4. The Role of SSS in Reading   59
5. The Role of SSS in Learning Disabilities   79
6. The Role of SSS in Dyslexia   95
7. The Role of SSS in Other Related Problems   111
8. Screening for SSS   127
9. Pinpointing and Treating SSS   155
10. Bringing It All Together   167
11. The Future   181

Clinics: Where to Turn for Help   187

Index   193

Acknowledgments

A new idea might go nowhere without the support and devotion of others. Challenging the established beliefs about learning and reading appeared at many times to be a Don Quixote-type quest. There are many individuals responsible for the acceptance of the Irlen method. To each one of you, thanks for riding along with me.

To Rudy Shur, whose idea it was to write this book and who offered the encouragement, vision, and opportunity to make it all possible.

To Bob Phillips, who has a wonderful gift of listening to my ramblings, taking the ideas and introducing logic, order, and structure. Your contributions to writing this book have been invaluable.

To those who had the strength to encourage me from the very beginning to challenge the present beliefs and systems and who supported me even in the face of opposition: Dr. Robert Swan, Dave Sanfilippo, and Dr. Gen Ramirez. You are my Sancho Panza.

To those individuals all over the world who have made Scotopic Sensitivity Syndrome a part of their life's work, your loyalty and your belief in SSS as a process that would revolutionize education have been my lance in the struggle to gain acceptance: Dr. Sheldon Pitluck, Dr. Mary Jo Lass, Dr. Paul Whiting, Dr. Greg Robinson, Dr. Peter O'Connor, Dr. Sue Fricker, Dr. Sheldon Beebe, Dr. Dale Jordan, Dr. Bill Hendrix, Dr. William Henks, Debbie Harris-Meek, Mary Davies, and all the professionals who have become diagnosticians and screeners to make this process available to thousands around the world. I thank you from the bottom of my heart because without your efforts SSS would still be just an idea.

To Joe Wershba, producer for *60 Minutes,* who made sure that others would pay attention. Joe, you treated those with SSS with dignity and compassion while making it easy for them to tell their stories of hurt, humiliation, and failure. You and Morley Safer stood up to opposition and told the story the way it needed to be told.

To Shirley and Mary, who have been with me since the very beginning. You survived the deluge after *60 Minutes* and put up with my disorganization. Your enthusiasm and commitment to this process are appreciated.

This book is a tribute to those adults who have struggled a lifetime with SSS, who have spent years not understanding why they could not achieve or why they felt like failures. You were willing to take a chance and share with me the types of difficulties you were having. If it were not for your courage and perceptions, SSS would still remain a hidden piece of the puzzle. You showed me the value of putting professional expertise aside and giving credence and significance to the information of those who have the greatest insight into their own problems. These words are your words!

To all the children and adults from all over the world who have written to thank me . . . thank you.

With love and devotion to my family: my husband, Robert, and my wonderful children, David and Sandra . . . I love you.

Foreword

One of the major hopes of lifelong educators is that now and then we will find a diamond in the gravel pit of educational experience. Occasionally such a remarkable discovery comes along. During my three decades of working with struggling learners, a handful of brilliant discoveries have occurred. This book tells the story of such a breakthrough.

Helen Irlen's contribution to the process of reading has made it possible for a special population to receive the gift of clear visual perception. My own work with Scotopic Sensitivity Syndrome has allowed me to witness the exploding joy that comes through suddenly being able to read the printed page. I have watched a generation of adults and youngsters weep with joy as the Irlen procedure has stopped moving print and cleared smudged lines to let strugglers perceive printed information clearly for the first time. This gift of clear visual perception through the Irlen procedure sets many strugglers free. Being able to read for sixty minutes instead of for only a few seconds at a time is an unbelievable experience. Being able to stay with a prolonged reading task without headache or painful stress is incredible. Acquiring stable depth perception and no longer being afraid of one's environment is blessed relief. Being comfortable under bright light without having to shade the page or squint the eyes allows relaxation instead of living with heavy dread and a build-up of anxiety.

As you read Helen Irlen's story, you will learn how she discovered the problem of Scotopic Sensitivity Syndrome. Hers is one of the most remarkable educational contributions of our time. As Scotopic Sensitivity Syndrome science becomes more refined, students of the future will not have to experience years of frustration and failure because of uncorrected visual perception that blocks reading ability. The Irlen procedure is one of the most welcome techniques of my lifetime.

Dale R. Jordan, Ph.D.
Director
National Center for Research of Learning Disability
University of the Ozarks
Clarksville, Arkansas

Self-Test

Do you or someone you know have difficulty reading? Take the following test:

	Yes	No
Do you skip words or lines when reading?	——	——
Do you reread lines?	——	——
Do you lose your place?	——	——
Are you easily distracted when reading?	——	——
Do you need to take breaks often?	——	——
Do you find it harder to read the longer you read?	——	——
Do you get headaches when you read?	——	——
Do your eyes get red and watery?	——	——
Does reading make you tired?	——	——
Do you blink or squint?	——	——
Do you prefer to read in dim light?	——	——
Do you read close to the page?	——	——
Do you use your finger or other markers?	——	——
Do you get restless, active, or fidgety when reading?	——	——

If you answered yes to three or more of these questions, then you might be experiencing the effects of a perception problem called Scotopic Sensitivity Syndrome, which can interfere with your reading efficiency. Now, for the first time, there is a simple method that can help people overcome this problem quickly and easily.

Written by a college student who wanted the world to understand the frustration of the reading experience for someone with SSS:

B's and d's look the same to me—

And so do p's and q's.

N's and u's I always confuse—

And m's and w's.

The page is bright. It hurts my eyes.

The words, they jump about.

Like little worms, they wriggle and squirm.

They make me want to shout.

The teachers tell me I must try.

I try! I try! I try!

It hurts my head. It hurts! It hurts!!

And then I start to cry.

—David Artuso

1.

Why This Book?

Millions of children and adults around the world are poor readers. Some have been specifically diagnosed with learning difficulties, but countless more are either misdiagnosed or not diagnosed at all.

A breakthrough for many of those individuals has been the discovery of a perceptual dysfunction that accounts for their reading difficulties. That problem has been named Scotopic Sensitivity Syndrome (SSS). Individuals with SSS perceive the world around them in a distorted way as a result of a sensitivity to certain wavelengths of light.

Light is the basic component of the perceptual system. But any system can become dysfunctional. For some, reading problems can result from an inability to take in and appropriately use light. The distortions of SSS are most noticeable when an individual tries to read black characters on white paper.

THE MAGNITUDE OF THE PROBLEM

The scope of the problem is very broad. Reading problems are found not only in the United States, but in many other countries. For some individuals, reading problems do not improve with remediation and do not disappear with maturation. Many children with learning and reading problems grow up to become adults with the same problems, and to the same degree, regardless of the time, effort, and money that is used to help them. It is not just a loss to society but a personal tragedy.

Since so many individuals continue to struggle their entire lives with reading and learning problems, education professionals have a responsibility to persist in asking questions and seeking new answers so that all children and adults can be helped. People from many different cultures have found an answer simply by "reading by the colors." Scotopic Sensitivity Syndrome is not the definitive answer, but it is one piece of the puzzle for some individuals.

THE EFFECTS OF SSS

Here's an analogy to describe the problem: People with SSS are progressing nicely along the road of reading and learning, but then they stop because a large boulder is blocking their way. They don't know how to get past it. They can't go under it, they can't go around it, they can't go over it. It sits there and hampers their every attempt to move on. They are unable to develop a strategy to conquer the obstacle.

Understanding SSS provides new insight into the nature of perceptual-based learning and reading problems. Why is that so important? Because individuals with SSS have not only had difficulty reading and learning, but they've suffered in other ways. Many, for example, have developed poor self-concepts.

Individuals who suffer from SSS carry a huge burden. Society creates a constant and continual expectation to perform, but that expectation just cannot be met when one perceives the world in a different way. When words run like ants across the page, when the page changes color, when musical notes dance around on lines that weave and cross, when cars disappear and reappear next to you as you drive, when you play a sport and the ball isn't where it's supposed to be, when stairs look like a sheer slope, when you are not aware of how others perceive the printed page or what reading is like for them, then you don't understand why you can't do what everyone else can. You might see yourself as a failure or even as a bad person. You might even feel you have cheated your way through the system. Those nagging perceptions can stay with you for a lifetime.

FAMILIES ARE AFFECTED, TOO

When a child has Scotopic Sensitivity Syndrome, parents also suffer. They might have difficulty dealing with the poor performance of their child. They might become annoyed because the child appears not to be trying. They might become frustrated with teachers and school administrators for not recognizing and solving the child's academic problems. And even if the school system identifies and labels the problem, they might still be angry because improvement doesn't always result. Most of all, they might be fearful. Fearful that their child will have to suffer just like they did. Yes, many parents whose children have SSS have discovered that this type of reading problem is hereditary. They, too, have to suffer, often needlessly and silently, through school and adulthood.

Parents who seem to have nowhere else to turn often end up blaming themselves. They keep trying new ap-

proaches at home. They might try to sit down and work
with the child, punish the child, or feel that it's best just to
leave the child alone. Then, if the child continues to fail,
parents feel guilty because they do not have the answer.
All of that does nothing to improve the situation, and it can
even harm the parent/child relationship.

The blame, guilt, and frustration often push parents
into seeking private help. They might not be able to afford
it, but parents who feel their child has ability and potential
inevitably will spend a lot of money, often with very little
return for the child.

DIAGNOSIS AND TREATMENT ARE ESSENTIAL

Why is it so important to diagnose SSS correctly before
remediating the problem? Finally being able to find an
answer through treating SSS opens the door for options
and opportunities that otherwise would never have been
available. What options? Think of the satisfaction for individuals who would now be able to read for pleasure—and
be able to read the whole book, not just bits and pieces.
Think of being able to continue on in education, achieve a
career, and feel competent and successful. That is certainly much better than some of the alternatives, such as
becoming a dropout or gang member, being difficult to
employ, or losing oneself to drugs!

Techniques for assessing, diagnosing, and treating individuals whose school problems are related to SSS are not
meant to replace present educational interventions. Unfortunately, none of the current methods have all the
answers. More importantly, none of the current methods
dealing with academic difficulties can solve all the problems of any one individual, particularly if one of those
problems is SSS.

Although there are appropriate remedial interventions
to deal with many types of learning problems, there has

been no way of dealing with SSS. There has been no consistently effective way to teach someone to read faster, to read more efficiently, to do less rereading for comprehension, or to read uninterrupted for a longer time.

THE GOOD NEWS

But now there is hope. A recently developed treatment for SSS uses colored overlays and lenses to blast the boulder away. In its place are a number of smaller stones that those with SSS have to step over, carefully, before they get to the clearer road ahead.

For some people, when you take all the debris away, there's a clear path. But for others, there are more rocks to be dealt with.

The method described in this book is not an alternative approach to learning to read. Rather, it is a treatment that helps people with SSS by eliminating perceptual distortions, which can be such an obstacle to reading and learning. Having good perceptual skills is a critical component for effective reading- and writing-based activities. Improved perceptual skills also enable individuals with SSS to benefit more from reading remediation.

HOPE FROM A NEW CONCEPT

This book provides hope for many who have always desired to be successful, who have been frustrated over needing to spend so much time completing schoolwork, who must forfeit social life, friendship, and recreational activities just to survive in the classroom. It lets them know that they have not been responsible for their poor school performance. It allows them to re-examine the demands being placed upon them and their inability to live up to those expectations. For some, it provides a reason for their lack of success and offers a reasonable route to produce changes so that instead of suffering self-defeat and humiliation they can continue trying. That reason for lack of success is SSS.

This book has been written so that those who are suffering from SSS, their families, and the professionals who are there to help them can all become aware of the concept of SSS and what can be done about it. SSS is not the cause of everyone's school-related difficulties. And even for those who can be helped, it might be only a part of the answer. But people in need of help should find out about SSS to determine whether it is the boulder that holds them back.

It must be stressed that the process you'll be reading about won't help everybody. And as yet, we do not fully understand why the special treatment described in this book is so effective for those who can be helped. Nevertheless, a great deal has appeared in the media—newspapers, radio, and television—about the successful treatment for SSS.

Why has there been so much international publicity? People who have been treated successfully for SSS have been thrilled to find that, after years of struggling and suffering, they have finally found something that works. Those who have been successfully treated have been so enthusiastic that they want others who share the same problem to know there is hope. People seeing the benefits of the identification and treatment of SSS, either on themselves or on others, are talking about it. Many have been desperate to share their news with the rest of the world.

However, the space or time that the media can devote to any given story is limited. So another reason for writing this book is to give detailed information about Scotopic Sensitivity Syndrome; what its effects can be; how it fits into the current theories about reading, dyslexia, and learning difficulties; and, most importantly, what can be done about it and where help can be found.

Media coverage can be both positive and negative. Positive, because people become aware of the potential for helping themselves with a method they otherwise might never have heard of. But negative, too, because many people have a tendency to shy away from "solutions" presented by the media, thinking frauds or hoaxes lie beneath the media hypes.

There is a lot of misinformation out there. Most of what the public has read regarding SSS has been through the media. The media might only summarize information, presenting it in a way that dramatizes the process. Articles might not necessarily explain SSS in depth, and that has a tendency to turn off educators and scientists.

This book will present clear information about SSS and its treatment. The book presents a new concept, showing that a perceptual difficulty, specifically SSS, can affect ease and efficiency of reading and, if it is very severe, can even play a role in moderate to severe learning disabilities and dyslexia. Finally, the book will inform the public, including those individuals who have tried everything and decided there is no hope, that reading by the colors will give many struggling learners the chance for success.

2.

Discovery

When people read of a new development or breakthrough they are often interested in what led to it. So where did the idea of Scotopic Sensitivity Syndrome come from? The theory slowly emerged over a ten-year period.

When you are a school psychologist, children are referred to you to determine the basis of their problems. You try to determine whether the problems are related to IQ, learning difficulties, behavior, motivation, or attitude. You test, diagnose, and report, and that's typically the last you see of those students.

During my ten years of working in one school district as a school psychologist, each child remained on my caseload until the teachers' evaluations and standardized test results indicated adequate progress. (Of course, who knows what constitutes adequate progress?) So when students were referred, they stayed with me until they "got better." That meant I continued to make suggestions to the classroom teacher and to work with the child—sometimes until they graduated from high school ten years later. I saw them year after year. That provided me a very interesting perspective regarding children with learning difficulties.

SPECIAL HELP IS NOT ENOUGH

After tracking children over so long a period of time, it became apparent that learning problems do not always go away, regardless of the time, money, expertise, and effort expended. Even with the best educational efforts, individualized remedial instruction, and private tutorial help, some children still were unable to make adequate progress.

Brian's parents realized by first grade that he was having academic difficulties. He reversed letters, couldn't follow directions, and was in the lowest reading group. His teacher felt that he was quiet and introverted, his problems maturational, and that he would outgrow them. Since he was social and popular at home it was difficult for his parents to understand or accept the teacher's evaluation. By third grade his academic problems not only were continuing, but getting worse. He was having a harder time reading, and comprehending and retaining what he read, so his parents insisted he be tested. His scores qualified him for special education, and he received years of special help from the resources program.

Brian hated being in the special education classes. It made him think he was stupid. In addition to special education, he had four years of private tutoring. He had two years of vision therapy, spent fifth grade relearning crawling patterns and using colored patches (educational theories popular at the time), and received "treatment" by being revolved on a rotation table. It finally got to the point where he didn't want to be different anymore. He was tired of the constant school, tutoring, homework, special help, and exercises, especially since nothing was making any real difference.

THE UNRESPONSIVE SYSTEM

For some parents, the difficulty is getting someone to believe that their child has a problem. It is very frustrating when the school will not listen to your cries for help. Sometimes, parents are the only ones who notice the problem. They make repeated requests for testing, but sometimes it takes years before the school district begins the testing process. Many times the teachers either do not notice the problems or do not agree with the parents' observations and concerns.

Valuable years are lost. Progress is held back. Learning is questionable. Homework is neither completed nor turned in, but the child gets passed from grade to grade, and no one seems particularly concerned, except the parents.

The parents see a different child than the school does. They see a child who gets up Monday morning excited to go to school, motivated, and full of good intentions to do well and get the work done. However, by the end of the day, the same child comes home defeated. By the middle of the week the same child feels so far behind that he or she stops trying until the next Monday.

The parents might never get help from the school district. The child might never get tested, and perhaps no one ever identifies an underlying learning problem. The result is one lost youth who grows up feeling defeated by the educational system. The child mentally drops out of school years before physically leaving it.

What are the options for such parents? Not many. When the school system does not recognize a problem, the parents must resort to their own resources. Some seek private help or choose home schooling as valid alternatives. Children whose learning problems go unidentified cannot compete or keep up with their classmates. They turn off in order to survive.

Josh is in eighth grade. His mother began requesting special testing when he was in second grade. The school finally agreed to test Josh's vision and hearing when he was in third grade. He was evaluated by the speech therapist, and the parents were told he did not meet the criteria for special education but could receive speech therapy and counseling. By fifth grade, Josh had stopped doing schoolwork. When he was retained in fifth grade his mother pulled him out of school. He was home-schooled and also took theatrical classes at a local college. At 10 years of age he was able to participate in classes with 18-, 19-, and 23-year-olds. Although he found reading difficult, he found it easy to memorize lines. He returned to school and received a social promotion (one for reasons other than academics) to the seventh grade. He would start out each week highly motivated and with good intentions, but by Wednesday he would be so far behind that he would not go to school for the rest of the week. His seventh-grade standardized test scores showed a third-grade reading level and even lower reading comprehension. When his mother confronted the school with those results, its only comment was that Josh didn't try when taking the tests. Eventually, Josh's failure in school led to his drinking and hospitalization.

WHEN LEARNING PROBLEMS ARE HIDDEN

Sometimes the learning problems are subtle. The parent, as well as the school, might be unaware that the child is in trouble. The child might cover up by working very hard in school and turning in all the assignments. The child might be given good grades even though the performance is below grade level.

Bruce's parents had no idea their child was having a reading problem. Because he was well behaved and tried hard, he received B's on his report card. But Bruce had to spend many extra hours struggling to complete his assignments, while other children had time to play, rest, and socialize. His parents knew how hard he had to work because they had to work alongside him for hours each night, reading assignments to him, having him dictate his work to them, and checking all his assignments before he turned them in. His teacher was not aware of his problems, because the school focuses on the final product rather than the effort it takes to complete the work.

THE MISLABELED CHILD

Many times when parents and teachers are unaware of an underlying learning difficulty, they misinterpret the child's classroom behavior. The child might be labeled as having behavior or attitude problems.

Susan comes from a professional family. Her father is a medical doctor, and all her brothers and sisters are college graduates. Since first grade Susan had always been in the lowest reading group. The others in the group moved ahead, but she remained behind. In Susan's words:

My parents told me I was a bright little girl and my only problem was not being able to read from left to right. I thought I was retarded. As I grew older, school became a frightening experience. I was in regular classes, and I wanted to do well. I didn't want people to make fun of me. My younger brother was doing well in school. My parents were

*proud of him, and I wanted them to be proud of
me, too. I began to live in a make-believe world
where my school problems didn't exist. If I didn't
get the grade I wanted, I would lose the paper or
doctor up the grade. I didn't want the teachers to
discover that I couldn't do the work, so I would cut
classes, go to the library, or sit on the lawn.*

*I often thought, why can't I read like other
kids? If I promise to work very hard, will you make
me like the other kids?*

Richard, now a successful businessman, had a great
deal of difficulty in school. He attended parochial school
and always had problems finishing schoolwork.

*No one seemed to understand what my problem
was. The teachers physically abused me because I
was not able to finish my schoolwork. My parents
did not understand why I wasn't achieving what a
normal boy should; they just didn't know why I was
having so many learning problems.*

He started behaving negatively as a way of protecting
himself from further hurts. He ran away from home,
didn't attend school, and had a large resentment toward
authority.

*I always felt very lonely and very different from my
friends. I couldn't seem to reach the goals that they
were reaching.*

WEAKNESSES IN THE SYSTEM

A number of things were becoming obvious to me. Standardized tests identify only certain children who have
learning problems. For every child the tests identify as
learning disabled, about twice as many are not identified.

A surprising finding was that many standardized test results often conflict directly with teachers' evaluations of students' learning problems! Some children who were referred for special education by their teachers couldn't be identified as having any kind of problem. But year in and year out, those children were not successful in the classroom. Teacher evaluations indicated that those children were having difficulty learning and keeping up with classmates. The children's problems had nothing to do with their intelligence or motivation. Yet, specialized help could not be provided, because standardized tests were not identifying any problem.

Debra was a C student who was not identified as having any type of reading problem by the school. Her second-grade teacher felt Debra was a little smarter than she tested to be. By third grade, both her mother and her teacher had become concerned and felt that something was holding back her academic progress. In school, Debra had difficulty settling down. She would get in trouble for giggling and not doing her work. She did not turn in homework or complete schoolwork. But she always started out each school year with a bang. She was always very excited and highly motivated.

Her parents finally forced the school to test Debra. Psychological testing did not determine any learning problems. The parents were told that Debra was very bright, manipulative, and undermotivated, and it was recommended that they learn how to motivate her. The years moved on, things got tougher, and she continued to fall further and further behind.

As I witnessed more and more of these cases, another thing became obvious. Even when a child is identified as having a learning problem and help is provided, that doesn't necessarily lead to appropriate remedial strategies or techniques to improve learning. There were many children who, no matter what we did or what was tried, didn't get better. It began to seem clear that we experts did not have all the answers. Many children with learning problems were growing up to become adults with the same severe restrictions on their ability to succeed in life.

LOOKING FOR NEW ANSWERS

In 1981, the federal government funded a research proposal for California State University–Long Beach to start an adult learning disability program. I became coordinator. The position provided a wonderful opportunity to research those factors of learning problems that had not responded to remediation, had not disappeared with maturation, and were going undetected by the school system even though they were often identified by the parents.

I began with three basic premises: experts still did not have all the answers; there were still unknown factors restricting academic progress; and children were not getting the kind of help they should, because the system was not prepared to look further than the range of options already at its disposal.

WHY ADULTS?

Adults provided an ideal group to study. Why? First of all, up until recently, most of the interest and research in learning disabilities focused on children. In working with children you can never be sure whether a learning problem is a true educational problem or whether it is a maturation problem. A variety of other factors, including teaching style, curriculum, environmental and cultural factors, and emotional problems, make it more difficult to isolate and identify learning problems. As a result, you can't be sure if a child is simply not succeeding because he or she is not trying hard enough. Also, with children, monitoring, recording, and self-reporting are not always accurate.

Adults provide the opportunity to work with people who are not usually intimidated by authority figures. They are accurate reporters, and maturation and motivation problems usually can be ruled out.

The adults in the research project were highly motivated. They were at least eighteen years of age, and some were in their thirties and forties. They had made it to college in the first place because they had worked two to three times harder than their peers. To remain in school, they had to: spend three hours reading material that would take anyone else less than an hour, develop compensatory strategies, and put much more effort into their work. All had been tested as having at least average, if not higher than average, IQ. They had learning problems, some of which were not diagnosed until college, and they had not improved academically as a result of any of the techniques tried on them to date.

What did the adults say? They had three major concerns: testing, remediation, and fear of the future.

Testing

Since as children they had always appeared bright and verbal, none could ever understand why they did not perform adequately in school. They were repeatedly tested, either by the schools or privately, because of the concerns of their parents. Since there are only a limited number of standardized tests used to identify reading and learning problems, they were repeatedly given the same tests. By the time I saw them in college, they had the test questions memorized! So not only was I not getting any new information, I was just reinforcing the whole concept of failure in the testing situation.

Remediation

Many of the adults were unwilling to undertake further remediation. Why? It's not that they were generally opposed to it; it's because they had been in remediation for so long, and it hadn't helped. They felt it wouldn't do them any good, so why bother? Both remediation and testing had the same effect on those students: a sense of repetitive failure. Both kept telling them that something was wrong with them. Said one of the adults:

> *I have had reading problems since third grade. They kept pushing remediation on me, and it eventually pushed me out of school. I started to not go to school in sixth grade. When I did go to class I blocked out the teacher and would daydream. I couldn't do it, so why bother? I felt like I was locked in a room. I knew there was something more outside, but I just couldn't get out to see it.*

Fear of the Future

The consistent pattern of failures was not what the adults wanted. They truly wanted to learn and be successful in life. They wanted to earn college or even graduate degrees, and they were afraid that unless something changed dramatically it would be impossible for them.

THE STUDY BEGINS . . .

After getting an idea of what I was up against, I planned the program. Any techniques that had been suggested over the past twenty years as being important factors in treating learning problems had already been tried on those adults. Many of the subjects had gone through special education, remediation, private tutoring, and other techniques, such as sensory-motor integration therapy, vision training, medication, and even special diets!

Hours were spent interviewing each student in the learning disability program and many in my private practice. Each interview was either video- or audio-taped for later review. During the period from 1981 to 1983, I interviewed more than 1,500 adults with reading problems.

Now it started to get very interesting. One subgroup emerged. The individuals in it had adequate decoding skills, good phonetic skills, and an adequate sight vocabulary, but they still found reading exceedingly difficult and avoided it whenever possible.

WHAT DID THEY EXPERIENCE?

Those individuals complained that reading was difficult. They reported they frequently lost their place on the page, read things that weren't there, and found that reading became unpleasant and frustrating. Not only didn't they like reading and couldn't do it very well, they couldn't do it for as long as they wanted to. Reading hurt! The page just looked different.

Some of the comments I heard repeatedly: "Reading is unpleasant. I become restless and fidgety." "I find that I fall asleep from reading." "I hate to read because I have to read something three or four times to comprehend it." "No matter what I do, I read slower than anyone around me. When everyone else finishes a chapter I still might be on the first or second page." "I can't look at the page for very long. I have to keep putting it down." "After a while I am just reading words that don't make sense."

QUESTIONING FURTHER

So what causes that type of reading difficulty? If we look at reading as a step-by-step process, then the first question to answer is whether the print on the page looks the same to everybody. I asked a group of proficient readers to read a printed page and tell what it looked like. All had the same basic response. They saw words and letters. They looked at me as if to say, "What else am I supposed to see? There isn't anything else there. Is this a trick question?" My problem readers were asked the same question. Most saw letters, words, and spaces, but a few reported things I hadn't expected to hear. They were saying, "The letters and words are running together," "The white spaces form rivers which run down the page," and "When I start to read, the words become a black line and I don't see them anymore."

After the proficient readers had read for a longer period of time I asked them, "Now what's the page like?" Again they responded, "There are words and letters." It was no different to them now than before. The subgroup with reading problems, on the other hand, all reported that things had changed and become worse after reading for a while. Each member of that group reported a variety of distortions. They had stopped reading because the distortions prevented them from comprehending the words. All their energy was going into perceiving the words or holding them on the page or even just finding the words!

Most of the students incorrectly assumed that everyone else saw the printed page the same way they themselves did. They had never had any reason to believe otherwise. For example, if when they read, the words on the page appeared to swirl, they might look over at their neighbor's page and see the same swirl effect. They just assumed that everyone else was reading a page that moved and could do it but that they were just too stupid or lazy. They felt readers had some special power over the book that put sense into it.

IN SEARCH OF PROPER TREATMENT

At that point, it seemed I had identified a problem that was holding back some individuals' ability to read. Unfortunately, those individuals hadn't yet gotten to the right professionals, the specialists who could treat their symptoms. So I asked for a group of professionals, representing a number of specialties, to evaluate and treat those students. Over the next nine months, thirty-five students visited a variety of professionals, including ophthalmologists, optometrists, developmental specialists, neurologists, reading specialists, and psychologists, and followed all their recommendations. Although some treatments were helpful, none made any significant difference in reducing or eliminating the reported distortions. None of the suggested treatments significantly improved anyone's ease or efficiency of reading. The final conclusion had to be that I was dealing with a unique syndrome that was not being adequately addressed by the professional community dealing with learning disabilities and reading problems.

A LUCKY BREAK

It still seemed that the goal was to stop the illusions and distortions that were so bothersome. Most specialists believe that problems with learning are problems with processing. In other words, the brain has trouble processing and understanding the information it receives. It seemed that an important part of the inability to process words on

the page was the instability of the words or the interference from the white background.

Now what? I tried a number of different techniques
over a six-month period. All were unsuccessful.

One day I was working with five students. One of the
students had with her a red overlay she had used four
years earlier in vision training exercises. Another student
put the colored sheet on the page she was looking at and
gave a little scream. It was the first time she had ever been
able to read without having the words constantly sway
back and forth! Each of the other students tried to read
with the red plastic sheet, but they found that it made no
difference.

I decided to try other colored sheets as overlays, to be
placed on top of the printed page. We went to the theater
department and obtained as many different gels as they
had available. (Gels are colored sheets placed over theatrical lights to color or soften their effect.) We had dozens
of colors spread over the floor of our room. During the
subsequent weeks any student who had reported having
reading difficulties due to perceptual distortions was asked
to try reading with the gels.

So what was the result? Much experimenting with
those colored sheets showed an interesting thing. Of
thirty-seven individuals with visual perception problems
in the study, thirty-one were helped by the colored sheets.
(And they helped fifty-eight out of seventy people tested
in my private practice.) For each individual helped, certain colors could make things better but other colors could
make things worse. But for each person helped, there was
one color that worked best. After everyone had determined and used their own optimal color, they reported
they were able to read better and longer.

When I tried the same test on the graduate students
who read well, they thought the colored sheets were very

amusing. After all, they just saw a red page or a blue page or a green page, but it didn't affect how long they read or how well they could read. Other than color, they didn't find the page any different.

Children were added into the study, and a number of those with reading problems also responded to the overlays.

COLOR ME LITERATE

The group of unsuccessful adult readers used their preferred colored overlays, or gels, for all reading assignments for several weeks. They reported back on a day-today basis. After the first few weeks, they described their reading as much improved. They were able to keep up with the rest of the class in reading, and they didn't feel like they were falling further and further behind.

After the fourth week they were still saying positive things. But they wished there was a way to use the overlays to take tests. They found that if they tried to use an overlay, they'd have to put it down to read the questions and lift it up to answer them. This back and forth actually created more problems. So they asked what could be done to help them take their tests.

The students explained that it was now easier to read books and that they wanted to take care of the areas where there were similar problems, such as chalkboards, overhead projectors, computer screens, and tests. They reported that, although the gels helped, they were still bothered when they tried to read under fluorescent lights.

WHY STOP AT OVERLAYS?

All of that information led to the next important question: If color works well as an overlay on the page, will it work just as well off the page? In other words, how about glasses with colored lenses?

I arranged for a local optical manufacturing laboratory to create a variety of colored lenses, or filters, in different densities. The colors that had helped most as overlays were not necessarily the colors that helped most as lenses. But yes, fortunately, the students could get the same or even better results by wearing framed colored lenses as by having the color down on the page. In addition, looking through colored lenses had even greater applicability because it helped the students work out problems directly on math pages, take tests and notes, read chalkboards, work on computers, and read for a longer time under fluorescent lights. They began reporting improvement and changes in many areas, not just reading.

Individual after individual responded to different colors. No one color worked for every individual. Preferences ranged from limes to roses to purples and all the hues between.

As time went by, I used more-sophisticated selection and measurement techniques. I used an instrument called a photospectrometer to measure the characteristics of each color. Each filter was categorized according to the amount of light transmitted for each color. I began to chart the colors of the lenses.

THE DISCOVERY GOES PUBLIC

In 1985, an Australian journalist living in Hong Kong saw an article about Scotopic Sensitivity Syndrome in his local newspaper and called me. We talked on the telephone. His daughter was dyslexic, and it appeared she might be a candidate for colored filters. He decided to bring her to the United States for testing. After the testing was completed and the daughter's lenses had been colored, we spent several days sightseeing. Every time the journalist looked at his daughter, she was sitting in the back of the car, reading. He said it was the first time he had seen his daughter read for pleasure.

During their stay, he questioned me about the availability of this process. He asked me how many people were aware of what I was doing. He wanted to know what I was doing to spread the word. He questioned me about how long it would take for people to learn about this concept. He wanted to know what I was doing to inform professionals. I explained that it takes ten to fifteen years for a new concept to become accepted by the professional community and be introduced to the public. He asked how this was proceeding, and I explained that the process was still in its infancy. My articles had not been accepted for publication. The inability to gain recognition was not as frustrating as the reason given by those reviewing my research. They felt that I was presenting research linking vision to learning disabilities and dyslexia. I was unequivocally told that this concept had been discredited years ago. They missed the fact that perception is not the same as vision and that I therefore was describing a process that had not previously been researched.

The journalist returned to Hong Kong with a determination to get the story to the public so that individuals could determine for themselves whether to try the process. The journalist and the executive producer for a television station wanted *60 Minutes Australia* (similarly named and structured as, but in no way connected to, its United States counterpart) to send a dyslexic child to the United States to be tested for colored lenses. I refused to cooperate. I felt it was essential that the story not be released in the media until it had been properly reviewed in the professional journals. After months of trying to sway me, they requested that I ask those who were directly affected.

I asked the adults who had been part of the research study for the past four years what they thought I should do. They said it was my responsibility to tell the public. They only wished I had discovered SSS sooner and been able to help them when they were younger. They told me it would have made their lives a lot easier and would have enabled them to achieve different goals. They felt it was essential to give people the opportunity to see the process for themselves. Based on those statements, I allowed the show to be filmed.

"Rose Coloured Glasses" aired in April 1985. I was awakened in the early hours of the next morning to learn that the response was so overwhelming that the television producers would be flying Dr. Paul Whiting, an expert in learning disabilities, to the United States to study the process, ascertain its validity, and be trained in it. *60 Minutes Australia* telecast his report via satellite the following week. Whiting returned to Australia to open the world's first SSS clinic, at Sydney University.

A short while later, producers for the United States version of *60 Minutes* were visiting Australia and were shown "Rose Coloured Glasses." They contacted me about doing a show in the United States. As tempting as it was to introduce SSS to the United States, I felt it was more important to train professionals to meet the needs of Australians.

On January 2, 1988, I was contacted again by the United States *60 Minutes*. They were still interested in investigating Scotopic Sensitivity Syndrome and possibly doing a story. I felt it was time to expose the process to the scrutiny of the public. I had appeared on many television shows in Australia, New Zealand, and England. Approximately 10,000 individuals had been tested for SSS during the preceding seven years, and professionals in education, psychology, medicine, optometry, and ophthalmology were supportive of the research and excited about the results. Some major universities in Australia and the California State Department of Education had completed research that validated my results. I felt better prepared for the tough investigative style of *60 Minutes.*

Its report, called "Reading by the Colors," aired in May 1988 and produced an avalanche of interest from professionals and the public. *60 Minutes* was overwhelmed by phone calls asking for more information, and the Irlen Institute received thousands of letters. Most of the letter writers expressed frustration over having known that something was wrong but not knowing what. Many were thankful for the television show because it showed them, for the first time, that they saw the printed page in a way that it was not supposed to be seen. For the first time, they had an answer to what had appeared to be an insurmountable problem.

3.

What is Scotopic Sensitivity Syndrome?

A number of individuals have reading or learning difficulties because they do not see the printed page the same way proficient readers do. They have difficulty processing full-spectrum light efficiently. This perceptual problem is now called Scotopic Sensitivity Syndrome. Some people use the word scotopic to mean night vision. I don't mean it that way. Scotopic Sensitivity Syndrome is a coined term. It's not the same as scotopic vision. Scotopic Sensitivity Syndrome has its own meaning and cluster of symptoms. Although little is known about the physiological basis of SSS, we do know that we are dealing with the spectral modification of light.

A PERCEPTUAL PROBLEM

Do you notice that I keep emphasizing the word perceptual? That's because it's important to realize that Scotopic Sensitivity Syndrome is a perceptual dysfunction rather than a vision problem, which involves difficulties with the functioning of the eye. SSS, like any reading problem, can occur with someone who is wearing glasses or even with someone who has perfect vision and doesn't need glasses. It's not going to be picked up by vision specialists, either optometrists or ophthalmologists, because it is not a weakness in the visual system.

When you're given a visual test, you're often asked to read a line of letters. If you have SSS, you might be able to read that line, even though the background is flashing or the letters are fading or changing shape. But if you try to read page after page of little print, SSS symptoms will start to interfere with reading.

Unfortunately, SSS is also not being picked up by the educational system. It cannot be readily diagnosed through currently used educational and psychological evaluations or other school-related tests.

THE EXTENT OF THE PROBLEM

For some people, SSS is much more than a simple reading problem. It can affect academic success, sports performance, driving, musical ability, coordination, and self-concept. It really has an effect on life! SSS seems to go beyond the title of this book, *Reading by the Colors*. But don't worry. It all ties together.

People might have trouble with many different aspects of their lives. The problems might appear to be separate, but that doesn't mean they are separate. For example, someone might say, "I'm clumsy" and think that's one problem, "I can't read music" and think that's another problem, and then add, "I'm not successful in school. I'm stupid—people are constantly telling me I'm not trying hard enough or I'm lazy. I can't catch a ball. Mom always yells at me because I spill things." Those problems might not be all separate. They might all have one source: SSS.

How do you know who has problems because of SSS and who has other types of problems? Other than going by what the person reports, you really can't tell until the person is tested.

WHAT HAPPENS WITH SSS?

How do you know if you have SSS? What clues are there? What does it feel like? What are the ways it can affect your life? Is it possible that someone you know or love has SSS? Questions, questions, and more questions. Onto the answers!

Individuals with SSS may experience any of a number of types of reading problems. Not only can Scotopic Sensitivity Syndrome affect reading itself, but it can affect energy level, motivation, and work production. In addition, problems with attention span, handwriting, gross motor activities, and depth perception might be a result of Scotopic Sensitivity Syndrome.

Scotopic Sensitivity Syndrome is not, of itself, a learning difficulty in the accepted sense. Rather, it is a complex and variable condition often found to exist as a component of dyslexia, dyscalculia, attention deficit disorder, and many other learning problems.

FIVE COMPONENTS

A person who has Scotopic Sensitivity Syndrome can experience any or all of its five factors: light sensitivity, inadequate background accommodation, poor print resolution, restricted span of recognition, and lack of sustained attention.

Light Sensitivity

No, this does not mean you are extremely afraid of getting a sunburn! It is a sensitivity to glare, brightness, and certain lighting conditions. Which ones? Besides fluorescent lighting, there can be a sensitivity to bright sunlight, haze, and overcast conditions.

Individuals with SSS often state that lighting is bright. They might find artificial light "too bright," with full fluorescent lighting often the worst offender. Some read with all the lights off. Although most people with SSS prefer to read in dim light, some prefer more light. Those individuals feel as if they never have enough light to read comfortably. Some individuals can never find the right position to read and keep wiggling, squirming, or changing positions.

When individuals with SSS read under fluorescent lighting, they might experience dizziness and a sense of agitation or restlessness that could result in headaches, even migraines. They usually prefer to read under dimmer or indirect natural light. They might try to shade the reading material from overhead lights. Light-sensitive individuals under any type of lighting conditions might experience fatigue, which reduces the amount of energy available for visually intensive tasks such as reading.

Individuals who are light sensitive experience problems with glare in their environment and on the printed page. The sensitivity to glare makes it a battle to keep the eye on the page and to move across the line consistently and effectively.

Light sensitivity might also result in difficulty driving at night because of streetlights and oncoming headlights.

A published author and playwright, Ayofemi Folayan, talks about her difficulty with fluorescent lighting:

> *When I wasn't sitting under fluorescent lights, I was so much smarter than everybody else. I could*

do math calculations in my head real fast. I could memorize things nobody else could. Once I figured things out, I understood them in a way that meant I would always remember them. For a long time I had no idea why I couldn't read or why my mind started to wander while I sat in school under fluorescent lights. When I was home and tried to study, I was able to make much more progress.

Part of why it was so frustrating was that I had no language to talk about what I was experiencing. I didn't know everybody didn't get a terrible headache from fluorescent lights. I didn't know that other kids could look at a page of print and the lines would stay neatly [instead of moving] at a crazy angle like worms trying to squeeze out the neck of a bottle. All these things happened under fluorescent lights and burned away my ability to think, understand, and effectively communicate. If I had known, I wouldn't have felt so stupid or so hopeless.

Inadequate Background Accommodation

This is trouble dealing with high contrasts, such as between black and white. (See Figure 3.1.) High contrast is supposed to be the best for reading because it allows the letters to dominate with no interference from the background. You notice the letters and nothing else. For those with SSS there is insufficient contrast between the black letters and the white background. The background begins to compete for their attention. The white can even become dominant, and then the letters lose their distinctiveness. The background can overpower the black, making the letters less readable. One student explains:

When I look at the page, I don't see the words. Instead, I am acutely aware of the white spaces.

*They seem to make patterns. Sometimes the white
background makes letters and I read those instead
of the [black] letters.*

A phenomenon called irradiation, traditionally considered a night phenomenon, can also occur. When it does,
the background becomes more pronounced and rises up
and seems to take over, or swallow up, the black letters.
The letters become thinner, grayer, or less distinct in
sections. Parts of the letters might disappear. One graduate student called it a "white-out effect":

Figure 3.1. What do you notice in this drawing? Do you see a
vase? Do you see silhouettes of two faces? Do they compete for
your attention?

> *Each word has a bright, white corona. If I concentrate on one area, the white spreads out between the letters and makes them disappear.*

The white can eat away at the letters. Instead of letters always looking the same, they can look different at different times. When people with SSS are reading, it is not unusual for periods, commas, and the dots on tops of i's to disappear. Letters become interchangeable as they lose their center or parts of their lines. Letters such as b, d, and p can be easily confused. Letters such as m, u, w, n, and h become hard to distinguish. Letters such as a, e, o, and u can appear to be the same. (See Figure 3.2.)

> *Reading is confusing because I'm never sure what the letters are supposed to be. Sometimes I see a circle, and it can be either b, d, or even an o. Most of the time I just guess at words rather than read them.*

Some people said the brightness of the page competes with the print for their attention. The brightness can interfere with their ability to concentrate and stay with the reading task. In the words of a nine-year-old California student:

> *The white is so bright and I can't see the words that good. The brightness makes my eyes hurt, and I rub them and blink a lot. Sometimes I move closer to see if that will help. The white hurts, and I keep looking away.*

Background distortions make it a battle to read consistently. When such problems occur, the person has to re-read the same material frequently. That reduces reading rate and efficiency.

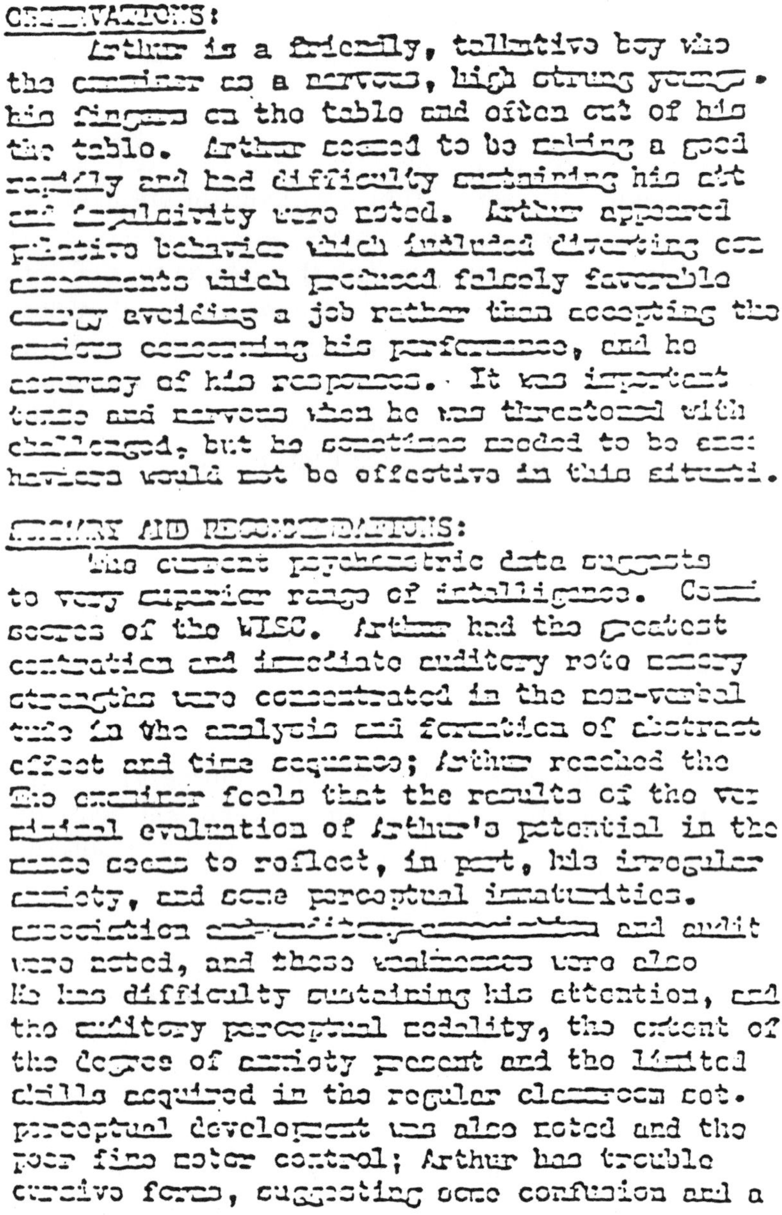

OBSERVATIONS:

Arthur is a friendly, talkative boy who
the examiner as a nervous, high strung young.
his fingers on the table and often out of his
the table. Arthur seemed to be making a good
rapidly and had difficulty sustaining his att
and impulsivity were noted. Arthur appeared
pldistive behavior which included diverting con
assessments which produced falsely favorable
essay avoiding a job rather than accepting the
anxious concerning his performance, and he
accuracy of his responses. It was important
terms and nervous when he was threatened with
challenged, but he sometimes needed to be enc
haviors would not be effective in this situati.

SUMMARY AND RECOMMENDATIONS:

The current psychiatric data suggests
to very superior range of intelligence. Com
scores of the WISC. Arthur had the greatest
centration and immediate auditory rote memory
strengths were concentrated in the non-verbal
task in the analysis and formation of abstract
effect and time sequence; Arthur reached the
The examiner feels that the results of the ver
minimal evaluation of Arthur's potential in the
range seems to reflect, in part, his irregular
anxiety, and some perceptual immaturities.
association and audit
were noted, and these weaknesses were also
He has difficulty sustaining his attention, and
the auditory perceptual modality, the extent of
the degree of anxiety present and the limited
skills acquired in the regular classroom not.
perceptual development was also noted and the
poor fine motor control; Arthur has trouble
cursive forms, suggesting some confusion and a

Figure 3.2. The washout effect.

Other things can happen to the background. Colors can appear, lights can flash like firecrackers, and the white can blink. It is hard not to pay attention to all the background interference. It makes reading a chore.

A business teacher in Chicago said he sees a white glow around every letter on a page. The spaces between the lines light up and produce a neon effect. (See Figure 3.3.) The different colored halos overlap, making it confusing to discern the letters. Lights flash all over the page. Reading for more than a few minutes is practically impossible, and looking at the white page with black print is physically painful. He experiences intense fatigue and excruciating headaches when he tries to read for any length of time.

Poor Print Resolution

This involves trouble reading print easily and automatically because letters, numbers, and symbols change. Problems include letters that dance, vibrate, pulsate, jiggle, shift, shimmer, move, or disappear. (Sounds like the latest rock group!) In general, letters or words seem to collapse into each other, turn around, fade, or just drop off the page.

Problems of print resolution depend on print size, spacing, typeface, and the amount of print on the page.

Therefore, it is understandable that in the third grade, when the print becomes smaller and the amount of print on the page increases, some children who had not appeared to have a reading problem will suddenly develop trouble.

Some of the letters or words the individual is reading might be stable, but the rest of the words on the page might be changing; or the words being read and the surrounding words can all be distorted. Reading becomes

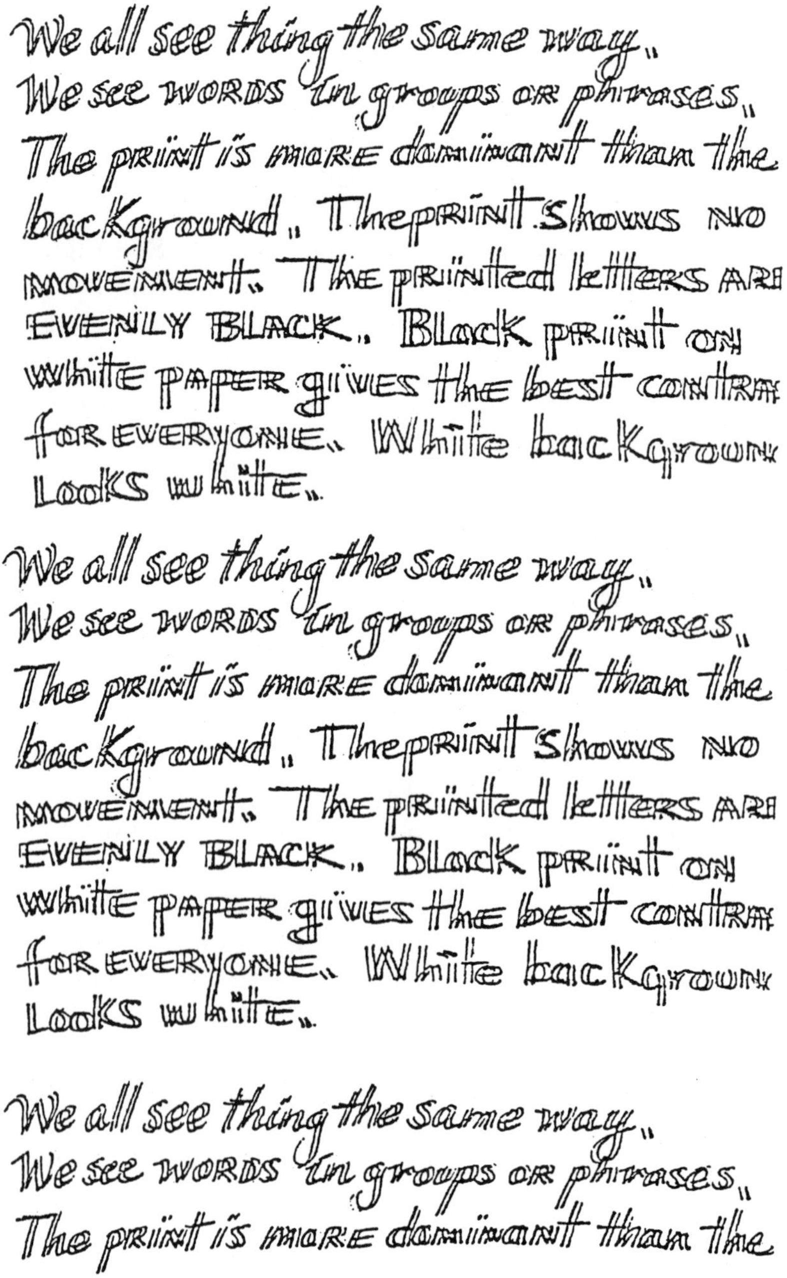

We all see thing the same way.
We see words in groups or phrases.
The print is more dominant than the
background. The print shows no
movement. The printed letters are
evenly black. Black print on
white paper gives the best contrast
for everyone. White background
looks white.

We all see thing the same way.
We see words in groups or phrases.
The print is more dominant than the
background. The print shows no
movement. The printed letters are
evenly black. Black print on
white paper gives the best contrast
for everyone. White background
looks white.

We all see thing the same way.
We see words in groups or phrases.
The print is more dominant than the

Figure 3.3. The halo effect.

slower, with more errors and omissions. The reader might have to go back more often to reread a vibrating word or a letter where only portions are visible. Surrounding words refuse to stay in place, causing the reader to have difficulty tracking, concentrating, and comprehending.

> *The edges of the letter are not straight; they look like someone had brushed them outward. They cross over each other and into the words in the line above and below. I'm not sure what I'm supposed to be reading.*

> *Some of the words do not seem to be on the same plane. They lift off the page toward me. Different words keep popping out at different times all over the page. I keep wanting to read those words instead.*

Besides letters and words that have unclear outlines, have halos, or lift off the page, words can have unequal or insufficient spacing between them and thus appear to run together.

> *I see a bunch of letters, but I cannot see where one word stops and the next starts.* (See Figure 3.4.)

> *Letters touch and cross over each other. The words seem to merge together. I do not see distinction of spacing between words. When this happens, I just stop reading.*

> *When I first look, I see a sentence; but when I try to read, the words all run on top of each other, and lines all mix together. It looks like one jumbled mess instead of a sentence.* (See Figure 3.5.)

Another type of resolution problem is where the letters appear to move rather than stay stable. Individuals report

However,bytheend   oftheday hehad decidedthat this
schoolwasbetter   than the   last oneeventhough   he
didn'tlikeit.   Nobodyhad   offeredto pullhishead
off,riphiscoat   orthrow   hisshoes   overtheroof.
on theotherhand,   nobody   hadspoken   tohimeither
By Thursdayafter   noon,   nothinghad   changedBill
was notentirely   surprisednoonespoke   tohimbecause
no oneknewhewas   thereeverydayhewas   witanother
group.   Heonly sawhisclasstogether atergistration
after thatthey   weresplitupforall   theirlessons.
Maths   withlx   Englishwithlcgames   with2yalesson
which   was   mysteriouslycalled   GSwithlz.Atthe
endof   that   periodhewasnowiser   aboutGSthanhehad
been atthe   beginning,Itseemed   thatthe classwas
on   page135   ofbook2whilethe   teacherwas   onpage
135   ofbook   3asbothbookshad   identical   covers
the lesson   wasoverbeforeany   onenoticed   Billhad
had nobook   anywaybeingadvised   toshare   withaboy
in   apink   shirtwhokepthiselbow   firmly between
Bill and   thebook.Whenthebellrang   Bill   grabbed
the   boy   inthepinkshirtbeforehe   could leave.
However,bytheend   oftheday hehad decidedthat this
schoolwasbetter   than the   last oneeventhough   he
didn'tlikeit.   Nobodyhad   offeredto pullhishead
off,riphiscoat   orthrow   hisshoes   overtheroof.
on theotherhand,   nobody   hadspoken   tohimeither
By Thursdayafter   noon,   nothinghad   changedBill
was notentirely   surprisednoonespoke   tohimbecause
no oneknewhewas   thereeverydayhewas   witanother
group.   Heonly sawhisclasstogether atergistration
after thatthey   weresplitupforall   theirlessons.
Maths   withlx   Englishwithlcgames   with2yalesson
which   was   mysteriouslycalled   GSwithlz.Atthe
endof   that   periodhewasnowiser   aboutGSthanhehad
been atthe   beginning,Itseemed   thatthe classwas
on   page135   ofbook2whilethe   teacherwas   onpage
135   ofbook   3asbothbookshad   identical   covers
the lesson   wasoverbeforeany   onenoticed   Billhad
However,bytheend   oftheday hehad decidedthat this
schoolwasbetter   than the   last oneeventhough   he
didn'tlikeit.   Nobodyhad   offeredto pullhishead
off,riphiscoat   orthrow   hisshoes   overtheroof.
on theotherhand,   nobody   hadspoken   tohimeither
By Thursdayafter   noon,   nothinghad   changedBill
was notentirely   surprisednoonespoke   tohimbecause
no oneknewhewas   thereeverydayhewas   witanother
group.   Heonly sawhisclasstogether atergistration

Figure 3.4. The rivers effect.

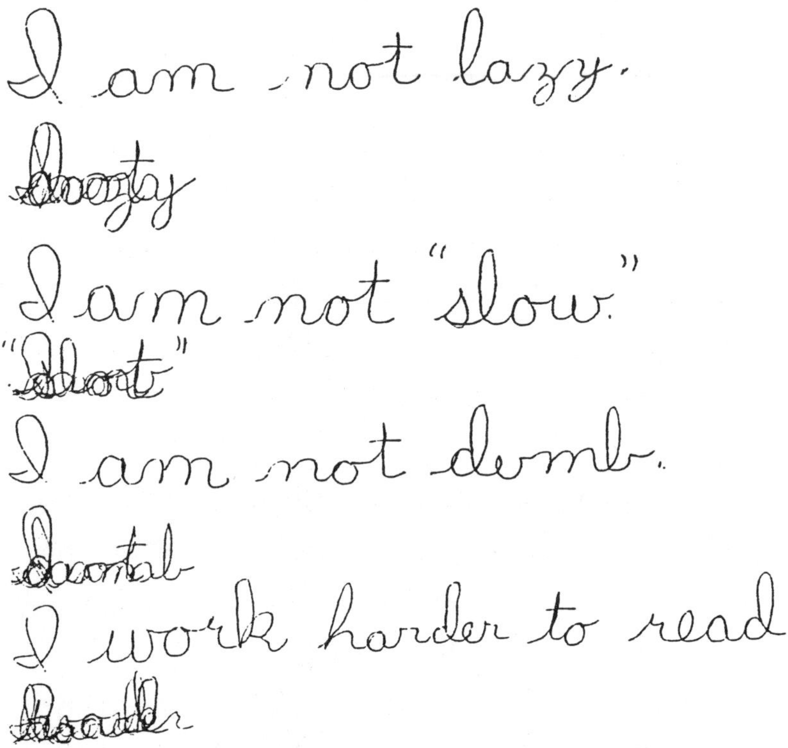

Figure 3.5. The overlap effect.

different kinds of movement, such as from side to side, up
and down, and all around. (See Figure 3.6.)

> *It is hard to read the words because they are
> bouncing around. The words run off the page. I put
> my hands on the side of the page, trying to keep
> them there. But it doesn't work.*

> *What words? What letters? I have black dots
> jumping and running around on the page. If I
> concentrate real hard, they stop moving long
> enough to become letters and I can read them.
> Then I'm off trying to catch the next dancing group
> of dots.*

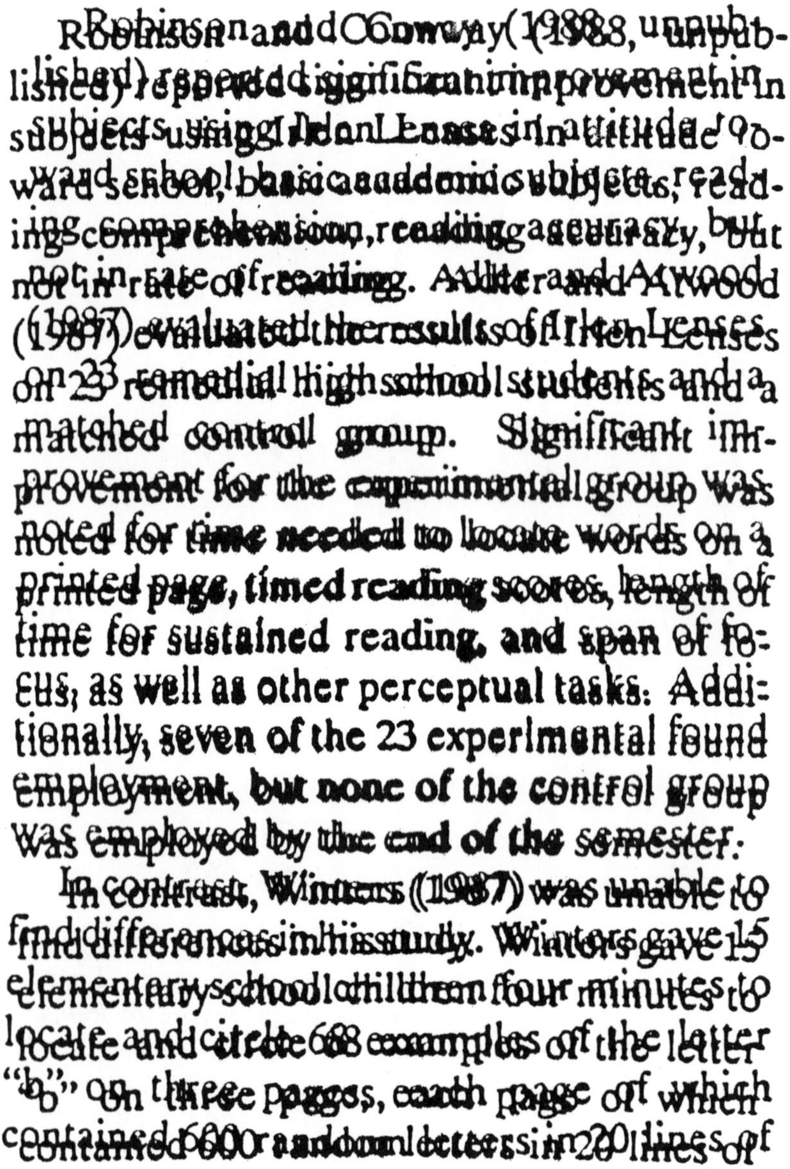

Robinson and Conway (1988, unpublished) reported significant improvement in subjects using Irlen Lenses in attitude toward school, basic academic subjects, reading comprehension, reading accuracy, but not in rate of reading. Adler and Atwood (1987) evaluated the results of Irlen Lenses on 23 remedial high school students and a matched control group. Significant improvement for the experimental group was noted for time needed to locate words on a printed page, timed reading scores, length of time for sustained reading, and span of focus, as well as other perceptual tasks. Additionally, seven of the 23 experimental found employment, but none of the control group was employed by the end of the semester.

In contrast, Winters (1987) was unable to find differences in his study. Winters gave 15 elementary school children four minutes to locate and circle 688 examples of the letter "b" on three pages, each page of which contained 600 random letters in 20 lines of

Figure 3.6. The swirl effect.

Letters and words can appear to pulsate. Instead of the print remaining the same in tone and intensity, letters can keep changing from black to grey to black.

The letters seem to be moving. The page seems spotty, and the words keep fading in and out. It is hard to distinguish what is on the page. I can only read a few lines before I have to look up.

There are different types of resolution problems. Letters tilt, stretch, overlap, run into the line above or below. Lines of print rotate around and around. Whole lines of print end up on top of each other. So many different things can happen all over the page, but rarely does just one distortion occur alone.

The letters have a life of their own. The print is not black but unevenly shaded, and the background is glaring. The words I try to read are not firmly printed on the page but seem engaged in a complex dance, and other words keep crowding in.

There are flashing lights blocking things out. Flashing red blobs obliterate the page. The print disappears, and assorted colored shapes drift over the page. Reading is harrowing.

The range of perceptual distortions is vast. (Readers wishing to view additional illustrations should see Figures 3.7, 3.8, and 3.9.)

Restricted Span of Recognition

This means that there is difficulty reading groups of letters, notes, numerals, or words at the same time.

Figure 3.7. The shaky effect.

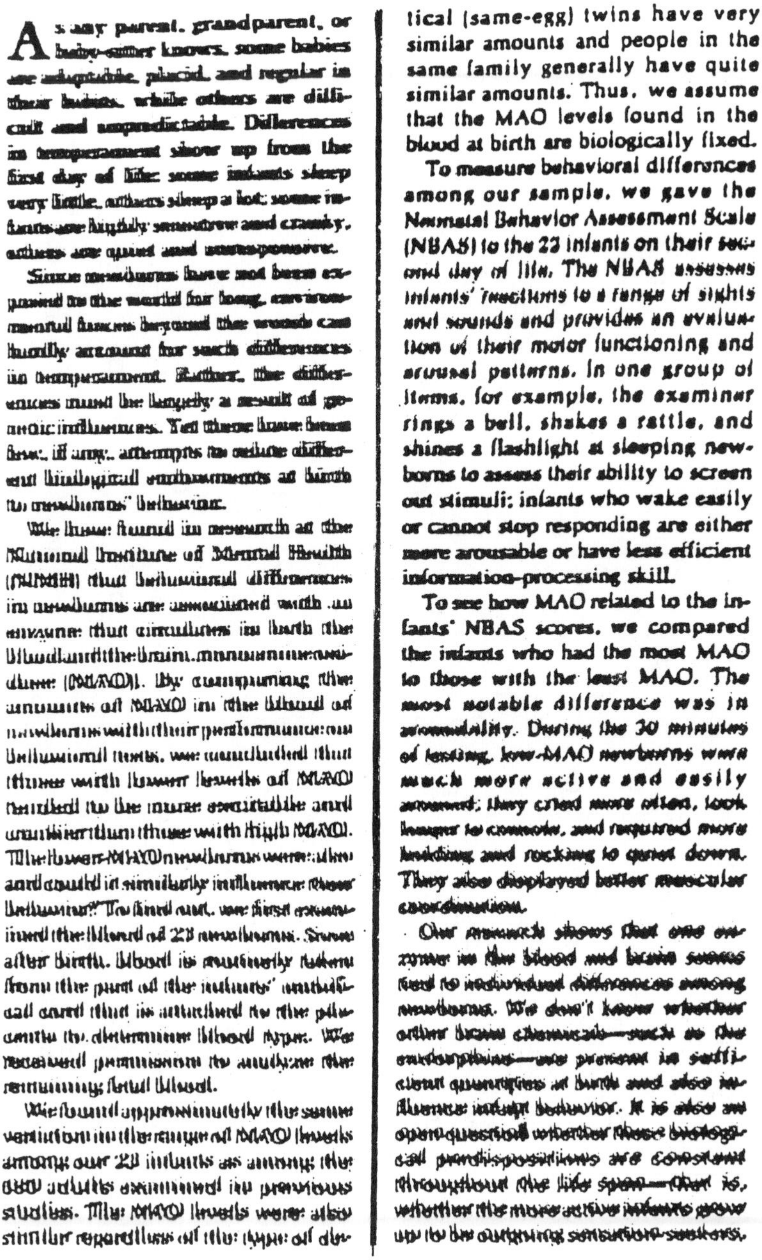
As any parent, grandparent, or baby-sitter knows, some babies are adaptable, placid, and regular in their habits, while others are difficult and unpredictable. Differences in temperament show up from the first day of life: some infants sleep very little, others sleep a lot; some infants are highly sensitive and cranky, others are quiet and unresponsive.

Since newborns have not been exposed to the world for long, environmental forces beyond the womb can hardly account for such differences in temperament. Rather, the differences must be largely a result of genetic influences. Yet there have been few, if any, attempts to relate different biological endowments at birth to newborns' behavior.

We have found in research at the National Institute of Mental Health (NIMH) that behavioral differences in newborns are associated with an enzyme that circulates in both the blood and the brain, monoamine oxidase (MAO). By comparing the amounts of MAO in the blood of newborns with their performance on behavioral tests, we concluded that those with lower levels of MAO tended to be more excitable and unruly than those with high MAO. [illegible] and could it similarly influence their behavior? To find out, we first examined the blood of 22 newborns. Soon after birth, blood is routinely taken from the part of the infants' umbilical cord that is attached to the placenta to determine blood type. We received permission to analyze the remaining fetal blood.

We found approximately the same variation in the range of MAO levels among our 22 infants as among the 080 adults examined in previous studies. The MAO levels were also similar [illegible]tical (same-egg) twins have very similar amounts and people in the same family generally have quite similar amounts. Thus, we assume that the MAO levels found in the blood at birth are biologically fixed.

To measure behavioral differences among our sample, we gave the Neonatal Behavior Assessment Scale (NBAS) to the 22 infants on their second day of life. The NBAS assesses infants' reactions to a range of sights and sounds and provides an evaluation of their motor functioning and arousal patterns. In one group of items, for example, the examiner rings a bell, shakes a rattle, and shines a flashlight at sleeping newborns to assess their ability to screen out stimuli: infants who wake easily or cannot stop responding are either more arousable or have less efficient information-processing skill.

To see how MAO related to the infants' NBAS scores, we compared the infants who had the most MAO to those with the least MAO. The most notable difference was in arousability. During the 30 minutes of testing, low-MAO newborns were much more active and easily aroused; they cried more often, took longer to console, and required more holding and rocking to quiet down. They also displayed better muscular coordination.

Our research shows that one enzyme in the blood and brain seems tied to individual differences among newborns. We don't know whether other brain chemicals—such as the endorphins—are present in sufficient quantities at birth and also influence infant behavior. It is also an open question whether these biological predispositions are constant throughout the life span—that is, whether the more active infants grow up to be outgoing sensation-seekers.

Figure 3.8. The blurry effect.

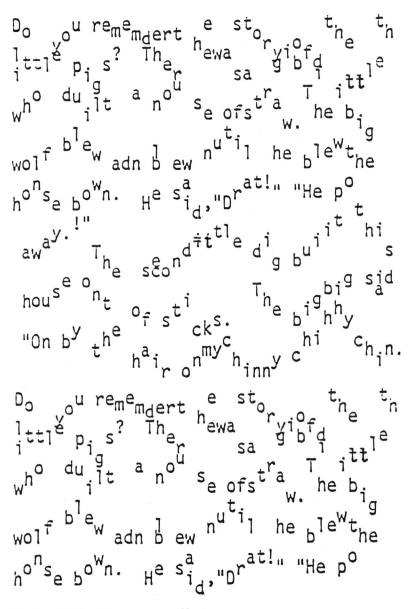

Figure 3.9. The seesaw effect.

Individuals with such a restriction, known as tunnel reading, lack the capability to move from line to line, to copy, to proofread, to skim, or to speed read.

Having an insufficient span of recognition means that reading books not broken into columns will be hard, and reading hyphenated words that begin on one line and end on the next will also be difficult. When teachers write across the whole chalkboard, they create more of a problem for reading and copying than when they write in short columns. The visual imagery necessary for spelling is nonexistent, and there might be an overdependence on spelling phonetically.

One adult, unable to graduate from college because of his tunnel reading, reported that reading was like placing a book on flashcards—one letter per card—then holding up the cards one at a time. He had learned how to get the waiter or waitress in a restaurant to recite the menu. If asked why, he would say, "If I had to read the menu letter by letter we would be here for days."

I cannot read more than one typed letter at a time. The rest of the page is just a bunch of black ants rapidly running around. It is so slow and tiring that I give up after reading a paragraph.

When I look at a word I can read the first three letters. It feels as if my reading is jerky. Move, stop, move. I just cannot increase my speed. I can never finish a test or copy work before it gets erased [from the chalkboard].

I cannot see more than one typed letter at a time. I also see halos of light around most things, including people, objects, words, letters, and pictures.

Lack of Sustained Attention

This is the inability to maintain concentration while doing tasks such as reading, writing, or working on a computer. Individuals with this problem find that they must work to keep words readable. Therefore, they take frequent breaks or do other activities while they regain the stamina or ability to proceed with the reading.

Many people make the assumption that reading is effortless. Therefore, it should be no problem reading for a long period of time, consistently paying attention, working steadily, and understanding the material, right? Wrong! For people with SSS, it takes energy and effort to perceive and process the words. The longer they read, the more difficult it becomes, and they find that eventually they will be unable to continue the task.

> *I know I read differently from other people. I keep having to stop reading. Sometimes I get up and walk around; other times I just look away for awhile. When I was in school the teacher would punish me whenever I stopped reading.*

THE RESULT OF THOSE PROBLEMS?

Reading fatigue! As a result of any of the problems that we have just talked about, some people with SSS experience physical symptoms such as headaches, strain, burning or watery eyes, drowsiness, or excessive tiredness after short periods of reading or writing. Individuals suffering from strain report that to continue reading, they must blink, squint, open their eyes wide, turn their head sideways, or close one eye. They might often change the distance of the reading material from their eyes. Any distortion or background interference can cause reading fatigue. What happens when the distortions stop? Fatigue stops!

*After I read a paragraph, words start to disappear.
I blink, and it is alright for a little while. Then the
words start to disappear again. First I get tired, but
if I keep trying to read I get a headache.*

INEFFICIENT READERS

In addition to causing reading fatigue, problems of SSS
can cause people to become inefficient readers. How? The
individuals cannot effectively utilize reading skills. Too
much energy and effort is being put into perception. They
are constantly trying to adapt to the print distortions or
the annoying and changing backgrounds. The act of perceiving becomes affected in many ways. Some individuals
skip words or lines, use a finger or marker to keep their
place while reading, block out part of the page, think they
have moved onto the next line but then find they are
rereading the same line, insert words from the line above
or the line below, consistently lose their place, experience
difficulty copying information, and frequently move their
head while reading a line.

A CONTINUUM CONCEPT

Having SSS is not an all-or-nothing phenomenon. SSS
occurs on a continuum, from very slight to very severe,
depending on the type, onset, number, and intensity of the
distortions.

The problem can be mild. Good readers might have
slight SSS without realizing they have a reading difficulty.
They might find that they are putting more energy and
effort into reading, that they need to incorporate frequent
breaks into the reading process, that reading makes them
tired, that they must reread for comprehension, that it
takes them longer because they are slower readers, or that

they are unable to skim or speed read. In other words, some people who have Scotopic Sensitivity Syndrome are good readers, but it's much harder for them.

When the symptoms in children become more severe and start to affect reading comprehension, those children typically become identified as learning disabled. For some people, one aspect of learning disabilities can actually be Scotopic Sensitivity Syndrome. But remember, somebody can have SSS and not be learning disabled.

At the extremely severe end of the continuum, the problem is more likely to involve dyslexia. However, only some of the people who have problems with reading comfort and efficiency, learning disabilities, or dyslexia have SSS. Even if an individual has SSS, other problems can coexist and need to be separately addressed.

At the mild end of the continuum are the good readers who have just a slight difficulty with comfort and efficiency. California educators who have participated in the Irlen Institute training program estimate that about 12 percent of the general population suffer from mild symptoms of Scotopic Sensitivity Syndrome. Moving along the continuum, approximately 46 percent of those with reading problems or learning disabilities have SSS, according to research studies in the United States and Australia. (Remember, SSS is not a learning disability. It is one layer that can contribute to learning disabilities. More about that is in Chapter 5.) Finally, at the more severe end of the continuum, where dyslexia occurs, estimates by Dale Jordan, who has made several studies of dyslexics, is that the incidence of SSS is 65 percent.

REVIEW

It's review time! There are individuals who do not perceive the printed page the way proficient readers do. They experience problems with the print and/or the background. Individuals with SSS can experience a number of symptoms, including:

- Words seeming to fall off the page
- Words moving together
- Letters reversing and rotating
- Letters switching around
- Background pulsating
- Background flashing and twinkling
- Background being bright and uncomfortable

Individuals who experience those distortions engage in more eye movements, eye regressions, and eye fixations in order to read. They might try to compensate by using only minimal clues to read each word, and that can contribute to errors in reading and poor comprehension. A number of reading difficulties can result:

- Slow reading
- Inefficient reading
- Tiring or falling asleep
- Inability to do continuous reading
- Reading-induced headaches or nausea

In the years since Scotopic Sensitivity Syndrome was first labeled, thousands of people have been identified as having the problem. As a result of assessment and treatment, they've been able to experience a major improvement in their lives. Much has been learned about the ways SSS can affect people. Most importantly, SSS is recognized as far more than just a reading problem.

WHAT CHILDREN EXPERIENCE

Most children with SSS are affected in a number of ways. But do you know what one of the most unfortunate aspects of the problem is? The child who is scotopic often has no idea that the way in which he or she perceives things is not the way the rest of the world perceives them!

Parents, teachers, and friends might want what is best for the child. However, consciously or unconsciously, they will exert constant pressure on the child to perform. The child unable to achieve success believes he or she—not SSS—is to blame.

Children have little control over their lives. When their teacher tells them it is time to read, they try and keep trying until they can try no longer.

When their parents tell them to do better on tests or work harder in school, they believe it must be their fault that they cannot do the work, that they cannot meet parental approval, that they cannot please parents, teachers, or peers.

They also suffer if they read aloud. It can be humiliating. Their inability to achieve well in school is very frustrating. And of course, poor grades on tests bring self-blame and tears.

As hard as I tried, the teachers would tell me to try harder. By my teens I had lost all my self-confidence.

But it is more than a loss of self-confidence. There are daily and hourly feelings of failure, pain, and frustration.

The pain doesn't stop as you get older; you just hide the pain.

When I think about my friends who get good grades, I feel jealous.

When I compare myself to my brother who wins

scholastic honors and is able to participate in after-school activities, I feel horrible and wonder why.

When I compare myself to those around me who excel academically, have time for friends, time to play, date, or just relax, I lock myself in a room and beat my pillow and cry.

PARENTS OF A CHILD WITH SSS

It's not easy for parents to watch their children suffer with reading failure (or with any problem, for that matter). Parents go through a number of emotions, ranging from shock, denial, fear, and anger to guilt, sadness, and depression.

One cannot talk about a child with Scotopic Sensitivity Syndrome without recognizing the frustration of the parents. Parents want the best for their children, including academic success. Sometimes parents find themselves engaged in battle with teachers or an educational system that might refuse to recognize a problem or deal with it. Instead, the school often blames the parents, saying the child's problems are emotional rather than educational.

SSS can also be found in some students in special education classes. Special education students have been identified by the classroom teacher as not progressing. Parents who have children in special education classes usually become very angry and frustrated with the academic setting because they feel that the needs of their child are not being met. They don't want the child to experience any of the same hurts and failures they had to experience. This also has the potential to become a battlefield between the parents, the school system, and the child. What happens? Nobody wins! Everybody blames each other for the lack of progress and lack of success. But the one who loses out the most is the child!

FINDING NEW DIRECTION

It's very difficult for parents to accept that their children are not doing well in reading or other academic activities. Many parents try to deal with it by saying, "Well, that's OK. I'll try to help him or her compensate for these problems by finding other areas in which to be successful."

Maybe, for example, the child will turn out to be good at sports. That would be great, but Scotopic Sensitivity Syndrome can affect one's depth perception. As a result, the child might appear to be clumsy or uncoordinated, which would make the child less desirable for selection onto a team. Sports, especially those involving use of a ball, therefore might not be the area in which the child rebuilds self-esteem.

Maybe the child has musical inclinations. What if the child plays well "by ear"? "OK," one might say, "let's start him or her on music lessons."

Unfortunately, Scotopic Sensitivity Syndrome can affect how well he or she reads music. The notes (a series of dots spread out over five parallel lines) might pose a great deal of difficulty. So a child with SSS might not be successful in music training.

How about art? Can a child with SSS draw? Yes, to some extent. But how well do you draw if you have perceptual difficulties? Children with SSS might not see figures in three dimensions, might not see the fine degrees of light and shadow, and might have trouble with perspective. So a lot of people who have Scotopic Sensitivity Syndrome have difficulty drawing.

So now we have a child who might be having trouble with academics, sports, music, and art. That is not too encouraging for the child's self-esteem. Parents are probably having a pretty hard time, also. But as unfortunate as that is, it's nobody's fault. That fact can be at least somewhat comforting.

WHAT ADULTS EXPERIENCE

Adults with SSS have already gone through a lot of punishment. They are probably armed with a highly developed set of survival strategies for dealing with the day-to-day problems that surface along the way. What kinds of day-to-day problems do they encounter?

Let's say those adults go to work by car. SSS can make driving feel like walking through a minefield blindfolded! Fear of changing lanes, turning, and inadvertently tailgating (faulty depth perception, remember?) make driving uncomfortable.

At work, tasks that colleagues perform easily and efficiently are much more difficult for those with SSS, especially when working under fluorescent lights. It is not unusual for someone with SSS to be fired for making errors while under pressure.

Adults with SSS probably try to avoid situations that require reading. After all, they don't want their poor reading ability to become obvious. But covering up is possible only for so long. It's hard to avoid every situation requiring reading. And what happens if a boss requests a special report to be read? Adults with SSS might take the report home and work on it at their own pace or have someone else read or summarize the report to them.

Therefore, adults who have SSS might feel inferior to the people around them. Those without SSS might have little or no problem reading newspapers and books. But for those with SSS, it is easier to avoid reading. It is easier to get the information from television and radio. But those with SSS still might feel as if everyone else has more knowledge, and access to knowledge, than they do.

Adults with Scotopic Sensitivity Syndrome can have experiences in many aspects of life that reinforce, time after time, feelings of inadequacy and failure that might have begun in childhood.

WHAT TO WATCH FOR

How do you know whether someone has SSS? What can you look for? Be aware of the person who tries to avoid reading, avoids reading for pleasure, or reads slower than others. You might notice a very obvious problem with continuous reading. The person might choose to read in dim lighting.

Children, especially those with SSS, might go to extraordinary lengths to find a position in which they are able to read. It might seem very strange to an adult to place a book under a table to read it or to lie upside down in a chair. But to a child with SSS, it can be a perfectly normal thing to do.

A person's reading can be slow and hesitant. You might want to ask the individual to read aloud. But be prepared. The person might have trouble tracking along the line. Words or even lines might be skipped. Words might be misread even if they were read correctly on an earlier line. You might cringe at how the person struggles to get it right.

Overall, the longer the reading session goes on, the worse becomes the quality of the reading. Perhaps the most unfortunate part of the whole experience is that after all the agonizing and effort, very little of what was read may have been understood.

WHAT CAN HELP?

Let's first talk about what hasn't worked. The perceptual distortions and the ensuing reading and learning difficulties of SSS have not been corrected by remediation, skill building, vision training, diet control, sensory integration therapy, or drug treatment.

For people with SSS, the brain seems to have difficulty

handling full spectral light, causing distortions of the print or interference from the background.

Colored filters change the spectral content of the light. That appears to stabilize the printed page and improve the individual's ability to process information about the world outside.

Colored filters can be designed to meet each individual's specific needs. There are almost a limitless number of color combinations that can be prescribed. Only an intensive diagnostic process can determine the correct color, providing maximum benefit. It is only with that specific color that improvements can occur in reading rate, reading accuracy, reading comprehension, sustained reading, and reading comfort.

WHAT CAUSES SSS?

Scotopic Sensitivity Syndrome—and the sensitivity to full-spectrum light that forms the basis of the syndrome— possibly involves a structural brain deficit involving the central nervous system. If so, then signals sent to the brain would be inappropriately processed, resulting in perceptual problems. For those with SSS, full-spectrum light would distort what is perceived and processed by the brain.

Of course, that is just a theory, and it is also unclear exactly how colored filters reduce or eliminate the perceptual difficulties characteristic of SSS. However, it is possible that the filters selectively reduce specific, troublesome wavelengths of light. If those colors that may be involved in causing distortions were reduced, then the brain would more effectively analyze and process information without interference.

The cause of SSS is unknown, but the fact that it exists in more than one member of the same family suggests a hereditary factor. The genetic link at least lets children with SSS know that their reading difficulties are not due to low intelligence or bad behavior. Also, SSS affects both sexes equally.

Although it might seem obvious that SSS has to affect one's reading ability, the fight to convince the professional community goes on. Teachers, psychologists, vision specialists, and other professionals are not trained to ask the questions that elicit an awareness of the distortions of SSS, and individuals who have the problem tend not to report it. Therefore, the professional community feels that the problem does not exist. Our system has a built-in resistance to recognizing new problems, be they perceptual, educational, or medical.

Another mind-set that holds back recognition of the treatment for SSS is the refusal to acknowledge that distortions of the printed page or competition from the background can affect reading ability. That position is held by the majority—by non-scotopic individuals who have never had to read in the presence of such problems.

4.

The Role of SSS in Reading

R eading is something most people take for granted. It doesn't seem so tough to learn. Children get the basics in the classroom. As time goes by, they learn more words, more skills, and eventually—they read! And how necessary it is. After all, you can't learn much about subjects such as history or geography if you can't read the textbooks, can you?

For an adult, reading is an automatic part of day-to-day existence. Everywhere you go, there are signs to give you information. At work, you'll need to read the endless pieces of paper with requests, instructions, or other information.

Yet, as easy as it seems to learn, reading is an incredibly complex skill, involving a series of written symbols placed together in a predetermined way. You must be able to perceive them properly, decode them, recognize sounds attached to them, and finally apply your language, reasoning, and intellectual abilities to give meaning to those symbols. Not simple at all!

Of course, if any of those basic reading skills are deficient, watch out! You're practically dealing with a foreign language! Our educational system tests for and remediates problems with virtually every one of the basic abilities just mentioned. Unfortunately, one problem goes unrecognized. Distorted perceptions of the printed page, a result of SSS, can disrupt some of the components required to read.

WHY IS READING IMPORTANT?

Reading is the basis for academic success and, in many ways, success in later life. It's very hard to get through the educational system without reading. We're asked to take in information from textbooks, maps, and graphs; to read tests and answer them; to read information from the chalkboard and write it down. We're asked to read math problems and answer them or to look at a column of numbers and make appropriate calculations.

People who can't read can't study information that they will be tested on. They can't pick up a book for pleasure. They're afraid on the job that somebody is going to find out they can't read.

A lot of adults who can't read say it makes them feel like less of a person. They just don't see themselves as successful.

WHAT SSS DOES TO READING ABILITY

Those of you who were brave enough to try to read the distorted pages in the previous chapter found an interesting phenomenon: your reading ability deteriorated! You had to work at perceiving, and that slowed down your reading. Sometimes, the print became so distorted that you couldn't read the words and found yourself guessing, misreading, or skipping over words and even whole sentences and paragraphs. What happened to your reading comprehension? If you had felt the material was important, you would have had to reread words, sentences, or larger sections of the material.

Your reading became slow and inefficient, but most of all you probably didn't want to read or wanted to do it only briefly. What about individuals with SSS? They expect the printed page to become distorted at some point while reading and to remain that way as long as they continue to read. How truly motivated and determined are readers with SSS! Those who know how easy reading can be would probably not read if they suddenly became scotopically sensitive.

(If you haven't tried reading a distorted page of print, try reading Figure 4.1 before continuing.)

A person with SSS cannot become a fluent, confident reader, no matter what the intervention, unless the SSS is treated. Distorted perception would prevent the person from gaining the comprehension skills necessary to understand and enjoy books.

Reading to people who have SSS will not result in their developing the habit of reading for pleasure. Reading must be fluid, effortless, and highly pleasurable before one can develop a love of books or acquire the habit of reading for pleasure.

No amount of courses in skill building, speed-reading, or study skills will help a person with SSS to concentrate longer, eliminate wasteful reading, or retain more information while reading at faster speeds. When SSS is present, reading will not become quicker, easier, or more enjoyable.

Understanding the way Scotopic Sensitivity Syndrome affects perception and reading requires an examination of those who do not have SSS as well as those who do.

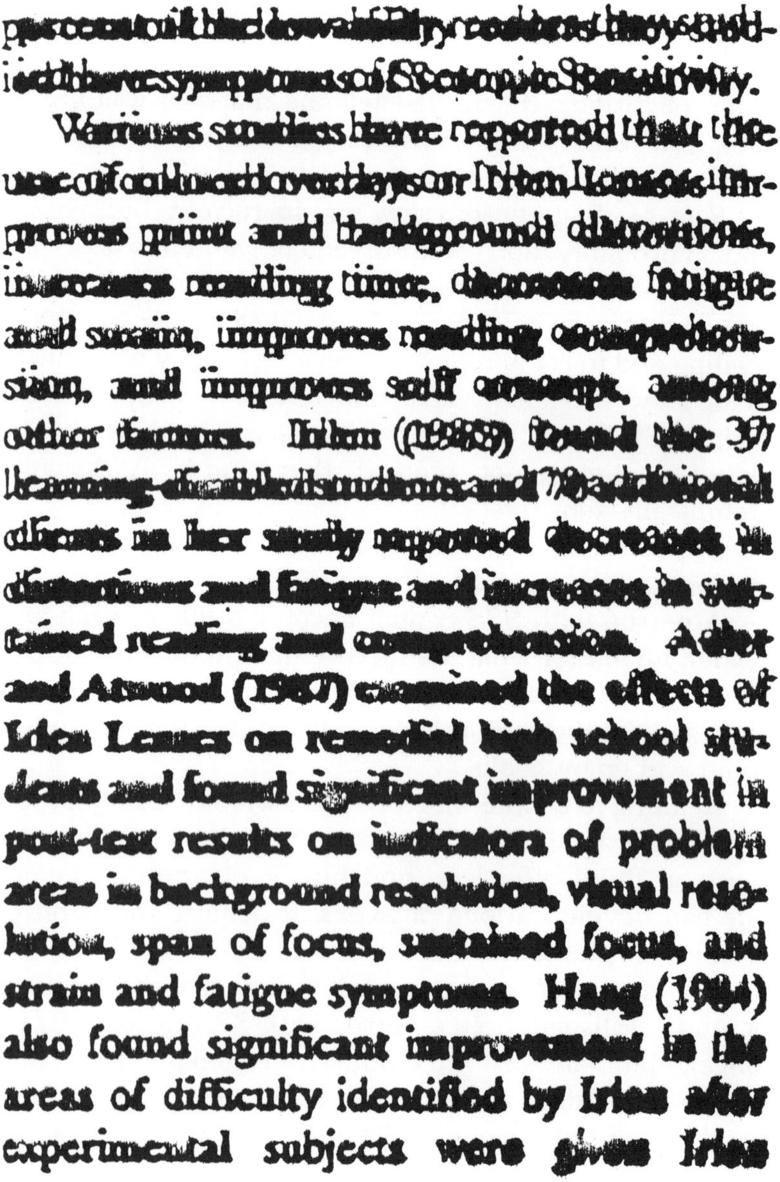

perceptual field toward... they studied the symptoms of Scotopic Sensitivity.

Various studies have reported that the use of colored overlays or Irlen Lenses improves print and background distortions, increases reading time, decreases fatigue and strain, improves reading comprehension, and improves self concept, among other factors. Irlen (1988) found that 39? learning-disabled students and 79 additional clients in her study reported decreases in distortions and fatigue and increases in sustained reading and comprehension. Adler and Atwood (1987) examined the effects of Idea Lenses on remedial high school students and found significant improvement in post-test results on indicators of problem areas in background resolution, visual resolution, span of focus, sustained focus, and strain and fatigue symptoms. Haug (1984) also found significant improvement in the areas of difficulty identified by Irlen after experimental subjects were given Irlen

Figure 4.1. What a person with distorted perception might see. Imagine reading an entire book of such severely distorted pages.

PROFICIENT READERS

Skilled readers are fluent readers whose word recognition is automatic, thus allowing them to use their linguistic skills and make extensive use of the printed page to gain information.

Reading should be an automatic process that takes little energy or effort. It should be a task that can be done for enjoyment. For proficient readers the task generally remains the same regardless of the type or difficulty of the material. Proficient readers prefer to read for long periods at a time and can read without having to incorporate breaks into the reading process. The ease and efficiency with which they read remains constant rather than deteriorating over time during one reading session.

For the proficient reader, comprehension is also an essential and automatic aspect of reading. Information is picked up from context clues. Words have meaning. Ideas are presented and then linked to form concepts. As complex as the reading process is, the proficient reader is like a champion skater gliding smoothly across the ice. Meaning just flows from the words on the page.

What about those individuals with SSS who do not become fluent readers almost automatically? What about those who do not develop efficient reading skills even with remediation? What about individuals who have the basic reading skills but cannot use them?

Readers with SSS have a great deal of trouble with their ice skating! They describe reading to be more like manual labor.

It feels like I'm mowing a lawn, and I just get exhausted and don't want to do it anymore.

A number of characteristics separate readers with SSS from those with other types of reading difficulties. SSS impedes the consistency and speed of letter and word recognition, forcing individuals to read material in a very different way. First, they might have to struggle to make out the letters. Then they try to string the letters together to form separate words. After that, they have to go back through the material again, to make sure they understood what they were reading! Those who have sensitivity to part of the color spectrum find that they put a lot of energy and effort into the act of reading regardless of whether they know all the words. Is it surprising that, under those conditions, the reader with SSS becomes restless and takes frequent breaks, whereas the good reader can happily sit and read for long periods?

For the person with SSS, reading can be a constant source of frustration. Not only is the printed page seen in a distorted way, but those distortions can make it hard to develop consistent word recognition skills, to use acquired reading skills, to read fluently, or to progress with remediation.

GOOD READERS CAN HAVE SSS

Unlike individuals with SSS who have noticeable reading problems, others with SSS are basically good readers who might not be aware that they are putting more energy and effort into the reading process. Individuals in that group might get good grades, but they probably put much more time into reading and studying than their friends do. They might stay up later at night to get the work done. They might spend less time with friends or participate in fewer recreational activities than they would like, because they need the additional time for reading and studying.

I never had time for anything but my studies. I never got to play football or baseball. I can't catch anyway, so I guess it's no great loss. I got a bit part in a high school play during the summer once. I would have liked to have done more, but I didn't have the time. Besides, you had to do cold reading to try out for real parts. I didn't even have time to date.

Many successful professionals have SSS. Many doctors, psychologists, teachers, and other professionals are scotopic but not severely so. For example, one medical doctor always got a headache from reading and just assumed that reading meant getting a headache. One college professor found that he couldn't understand the material he read unless he reread it several times. He compensated by recording while he read aloud and then playing the tape back to himself, thereby getting the information he needed while reading only once. And that's how he successfully completed high school and college and earned his doctorate degree.

If we persist in looking at reading performance in the typical way, then many perceptual-based reading problems will continue to go undetected. Some people with those problems might get acceptable grades but will see themselves as failures. They might feel that their inability to score high grades is their own fault, that they just do not try hard enough.

READING: MORE THAN BASIC SKILLS

Reading is more than learning reading skills. One must effectively use those skills. Perceptual problems such as SSS can be one reason that reading abilities are not used properly or do not progress. But the problem might be mistaken for poor motivation, a lack of intelligence, or a bad attitude.

If children are having reading difficulties, the misconception is that it's because they do not know the word or are having difficulty sounding it out. But few teachers check if that is true. How many teachers have ever asked a child who stumbled over a word, "What happened that made you stumble?" Only the person who is reading has that information.

People can stumble over a word for a variety of reasons, such as a weak sight vocabulary or poor decoding skills. But it's not always because they can't read the word. Sometimes they have trouble because the words on the page are sliding into each other or because they're waiting for words that have undergone the white-out effect to revert to normal. Those reasons are related to Scotopic Sensitivity Syndrome. But unless the right questions are asked of readers experiencing problems, all problems will get classified the same—as reading failure.

UNSTABLE READING PROCESS

The way reading is taught has been based too often on the assumption that the reading process doesn't deteriorate.

However, if a person has SSS, reading isn't a dependable process. The background can constantly interfere or the words on the page can come alive. Once those things start to change on the page, they get worse and worse. Things will become more severe as long as that person continues to read. The only way to stop the deterioration is to stop reading. When reading resumes, the deterioration probably will happen again.

I hate to read because it's such a struggle. For the first page everything is just fine, and I am able to understand what I'm reading. Then the words start to pulsate, and after a few more pages the middle of the word swims around while the rest of the words on the page keep pulsating. The longer I try to read, the more things pulsate, swirl, and switch around. I get up and get some coffee. When I return, I can read for a short while before the swirling and switching starts all over again. Finally, I give up. It is just too much work.

UNSUSTAINABLE READING

The demands of the educational system are based on the expectation that everyone can read for the same length of time. For example, classes are scheduled for a certain time, often forty-five minutes or an hour, during which the child is expected to be able to read, write, and copy. The reader is expected to be able to continue reading as long as needed to get the necessary information, to complete assignments, and to keep up with the class.

But those expectations cannot be met by many people with SSS. Their reading skills and sight vocabulary can be adequate, but their ability to do sustained reading can vary significantly from individual to individual. Those with the most severe perceptual problems find they can read no more than a paragraph or two (for some a word or two) before they must stop. Generally, those with SSS can read for about fifteen to twenty minutes before finding that their reading is falling apart. That obviously is not long enough to keep up with the reading and writing demands of the classroom.

Does practice help those with SSS? Actually, practice makes it worse; the longer they try to read, the worse the distortions and the less their comprehension. With SSS, it is not true that the best way for poor readers to overcome their difficulties is to read more.

DOES MATURATION HELP WITH READING?

The amount of required reading increases each year for children in school. The assumption is that with maturation, the child is going to be able to read longer. What is expected in the third grade differs from what is expected in the fifth.

A proficient reader can usually handle those increases by growing into them. But for people who are spectrally sensitive, the obstacle to efficient reading is always there. It doesn't change. Their skills, the length of time they can read, and their efficiency do not improve as they mature. No matter how much they try to work on their reading, they can't improve it.

> *Even though I'm now a teacher, a reading teacher, I still find that I can't read any longer than when I was in elementary school. I still can't read as long as everyone else..I just thought it was something that I was doing wrong.*

PHYSICAL EFFECTS

Almost never are those with reading problems questioned about whether reading is comfortable. It is assumed that reading is equally comfortable for everyone. In reality, there are some for whom reading is very painful. There are actual physical symptoms that can be associated with reading. People get headaches from reading, they get nauseous, they become drowsy, they experience strain and fatigue. One reason proficient readers can read for long periods is because they rarely find reading accompanied by pain, strain, or fatigue.

Because of those negative physical symptoms, an individual with SSS might, at best, read only briefly or, at worst, decide not to read at all. If you knew that reading for five minutes would likely give you a headache, for example, you'd probably decide to read for about three or four minutes and then stop. You certainly wouldn't want to have a headache every day or every time you read. You'd probably avoid doing something that causes physical problems, if you could.

Children normally don't complain of headaches. In general, when a child reports that reading gives him or her a headache, the adult's assumption is that it is just the child's way of creating an excuse to get out of reading. The child's complaint might not be given the credibility it deserves.

We know, however, that certain distortions can cause physical problems. For example, when David starts to read, words sway right and left. After a few pages, words start to twist and break up while the white background blinks on and off like Christmas lights. After a few more pages, the white background appears so bright that David feels as if someone is shining a flashlight in his eyes.

The white comes up and hits me. I feel like I've been smacked in the face.

That sense of brightness increases the longer he reads, causing strain and headaches. The continuous movement of words causes David to feel nauseous.

Why do some people become drowsy or fall asleep from reading? That is the body's way of avoiding pain. The systems of people with SSS can shut down as a result of the extreme stress of reading. It is understandable that one becomes tired when trying to read with lights blinking, words rotating, or a multitude of other things happening on the page.

TAKING BREAKS

There are strategies people use so they will be able to continue reading. One strategy is to incorporate frequent breaks into the reading.

A break can be as simple as briefly looking up from the

page or as involved as getting up, walking around, and not returning for five to ten minutes. It is easy to determine how severely affected an individual's reading is by looking at the frequency and length of the breaks. Those most severely affected take frequent breaks that get longer and longer while the reading time between breaks gets shorter and shorter. Some individuals keep a television on while they read so that they can take breaks every few minutes.

Incorporating breaks into the reading can help, but it also slows down the reading process. Eventually, break times can become longer than reading times. Individuals who cannot read a full chapter without stopping frequently will find reading a much longer process than their peers find it.

Those individuals who cannot read a chapter straight through do not stop only at the end of chapters or at the end of concepts. The breaks occur when perceptual distortion or strain interferes with reading comprehension. Those readers take a break, hoping the distortion or fatigue will disappear. Sometimes it does, for a short period of time. But since the breaks often occur at inopportune times, to return to the task of reading requires a significant amount of rereading and effort.

Adults with SSS are not the only ones who need to take breaks to be able to continue to read. Children with SSS try to employ that strategy in the classroom. When the child puts his or her head down on the desk, looks out the window, talks to a neighbor, or gets up and walks around, the child is often mislabeled as inattentive, distractible, or unmotivated. Quickly such children find that they may not take breaks, but neither can they keep reading. Many find that the safe approach in the classroom is to pretend to read. They move their heads from side to side and turn pages when those around them do likewise. Their behavior serves a purpose; it keeps them out of trouble. However, it does not help them to read or do classroom assignments.

These assumptions about reading are inappropriate for those with SSS: you can read for understanding even when basic reading skills are poor; skimming, speed-reading, and proofreading are automatically acquired skills; having students read aloud is a good way to teach reading; using a finger or marker while reading should be discouraged, because it encourages laziness and inattention and because good readers don't do it; fidgeting and inattention during reading and writing indicate a neurological abnormality known as attention deficit disorder; remediation can always improve basic reading skills; and children will naturally learn the reading process as they become developmentally ready. So many of the things people say all too often about reading are just not universally true!

ENVIRONMENT CONTRIBUTES TO PROBLEM

And if things weren't bad enough, it seems that the problems affecting the reader with SSS are made worse by certain environmental factors. For example, the level and type of lighting where one reads can speed up the onset of SSS symptoms and actually worsen the problems occuring on a page.

Fluorescent light is the worst of all. Wonderful. The kind of lighting most frequently used in classrooms and in the workplace is fluorescent. How much more difficult for people with SSS does it have to be?

In general, it takes more energy and effort for people with SSS than for those without it to concentrate and read under fluorescent lighting, and it requires more effort and energy on their part to read under fluorescent light than under any other type of lighting. They might be able to do it, but the price they pay is that it affects comprehension, the length of time they can read, and their energy level.

Adults with SSS often take their work-related reading home, where they can read under dim lighting—but children in school must read and take tests under fluorescent lights.

WHAT ABOUT MATERIALS?

Reading materials themselves compound the problem. The brightness of white chalkboards can make matters worse. So can high-gloss white paper. Both produce glare and make it even harder for children with SSS to stay with a reading task.

The amount of words on a page and the style and size of the print can also add to the problem. Many textbooks and magazines are more difficult to read than paperback books, which use no-glare, off-white pages. Books with pictures, large-print books, and books with two or more columns per page are easier to read.

Some students had, on their own, discovered they could reduce contrast on the printed page by highlighting the whole page instead of highlighting or underlining only key words. Full-page highlighting changed the white background to turquoise, yellow, or rose. Some students blocked out the page by using cards with windows to read through, and others spread out their hands or folded the page in half.

ASSESSING READING ABILITY

Reading difficulties have basically been defined by standardized reading tests. Those instruments look for very specific types of problems, primarily in comprehension, encoding and decoding skills, and sight vocabulary. But reading encompasses many more skills than those. Which skills? Critical thinking, analytical reading skills, and reasoning abilities, among others, are crucial to reading.

Standardized tests, at best, are able to diagnose accurately only a percentage of those with learning or reading problems. It is well recognized in the education system that only a portion of those students who actually need help are identified by those tests and thus receive help. Some students, for example, can read with accuracy long enough to be somewhat successful on standardized reading tests, but they cannot sustain their reading for the time it takes to do well in school or on the job.

Another area that is not properly considered is the complex concept of comprehension. The types of comprehension difficulties experienced by people with SSS are different from those assessed by reading tests. They are more subtle in nature and can even be covered up for short periods of time. There are people with SSS who are highly successful on reading tests and whose results suggest they have good comprehension. But, in fact, it takes them a lot of rereading for that good comprehension. They might be able to do well on a test, but their reading fails them in the real world, which often requires much more extensive reading and invokes the law of diminishing returns: With each rereading, the person can derive less comprehension as the SSS symptoms get more severe. And then time runs out. Or at some point it takes so much energy and effort that they stop.

The educational system does not quantify or even look at the energy and effort involved in learning. But without that, it's not getting the full picture.

I can read. I do well in school. No one thinks I have a reading problem, but I know I do. It takes me so much longer than my friends to finish a reading assignment. I keep losing my place on the page, reading words that aren't there, skipping lines so that I must go back over the material again and again just to read it right. No one knows my prob-

*lem, because I do so well in school. I just wish that
reading didn't mean I would get so mixed up and
confused by the page that I would have to read and
reread.*

The successful use of coping strategies can make the
accurate identification of a problem difficult. Strategies
can cover up what is going on. Some children are able to
pass standardized tests and get by in school because they
have developed an interesting strategy called skip reading. They learn how to get in and out of reading material
as fast as they can. They get only bits and pieces of
information. They might read beginnings and endings of
paragraphs. They might read the questions and then read
what they hope to be key sentences, and then skip onto
the next paragraph or maybe the next page. That is how
they survive. They might never have read anything in its
entirety. They might even pass reading tests and standardized tests. On the other hand, they do not really
understand the material. They grab just enough information to pass, but their reading inadequacies get covered
up.

SSS: A PIECE OF THE PUZZLE

The use of colored overlays, filters, or other aids as treatment for Scotopic Sensitivity Syndrome is not meant to
replace reading remediation. Rather, the purpose is to
eliminate the perceptual problems that inhibit the learning process. SSS might be only one of several layers
contributing to reading problems.

The use of colored overlays or filters will not alleviate
difficulties with blending, phonetics, or sounding out
words; nor will it increase weak sight vocabularies. But at
least now, with the distortions eliminated, remediation can
attack those problems without the interference of SSS.

The problem is that if a child is having perceptual difficulties, progress with any reading method will be limited. The student will be able to progress just so far and no further. However, the good news is that once treatment eliminates the problems of SSS, available educational interventions can help advance the child's reading achievement.

A number of reading methods currently used in schools can successfully treat reading problems. The success of an approach depends on how well it fits the child's learning style and needs. No one method works for every child, because the cause of reading difficulties can differ from child to child. Approaches include:

- *Phonetics.* Isolated letter sounds or letter clusters are taught sequentially and blended to form words.
- *Linguistic Method.* Patterns of letters or words are taught and combined to form words or sentences.
- *Orton–Guillingham Method.* A combination of phonetics and tactile stimulation is taught by using writing and tracing activities. The method works well for children with visual or auditory weakness.
- *Whole-Word Approach.* Before a story is read, new words are presented on flash cards and in sentences with accompanying pictures. The method stresses a contextual and conceptual approach. Children who make a mistake while reading are not stopped and asked to correct the word; instead, they complete the passage to concentrate on overall meaning.
- *Language Experience Approach.* Students read stories that they have written.
- *Fernald Method.* Students pronounce each sound of new words as they trace over them with the index fingers of their writing hands.
- *Choral Reading.* Students read aloud in groups.

- *Recorded Book.* Students listen two or three times to brief recordings of books. They visually follow the words, then read the selection aloud.
- *Paired Reading Method.* Parent and child read aloud together. Usually the child also points to the words and turns the pages.

CAN READING TESTS MEASURE IMPROVEMENT?

If reading progress is measured by looking at test scores (which measure only specific aspects of reading), then how can the effectiveness of SSS treatment be verified?

Sometimes, individuals with SSS skip words, read the wrong line, or appear to have difficulty reading words or sounding out new ones. The identification of SSS, and the use of colored filters, will indirectly serve to improve those aspects of reading. But what has really happened? Those individuals have adequate reading skills but had been unable to use them because of the perceptual distortions or background competition they experienced when trying to read. An individual might have appeared to be misreading or hesitating over many words in a paragraph, but what was really affecting the recognition and reading of those words was an inability to perceive the words on the page consistently! In those cases, a reading test given after treatment for SSS would show improvement that is obvious and recordable.

On the other hand, what about the individual whose reading is hampered by an inability to learn phonetics, by poor memory for retaining sight words, and also by SSS? In that instance, after SSS is identified and corrected, reading problems will remain and scores on reading tests might not immediately improve. Yet, if you asked that individual if the colored filters made a difference in reading, you would still get an emphatic positive response. The individual might report that reading skills are still poor, but at least reading is less laborious and can be done for longer periods of time. Since reading is no longer painful, concentration can last longer. That provides an opportunity to pay attention and work harder at building their reading skills.

Finally, what about the good readers with SSS, the ones who don't show any identifiable reading problems? For the good readers, test scores might not change, but treatment for SSS can present them with new options. How did they become good readers? They had to develop strategies that allowed them to gain information but not necessarily to read. But they didn't have any other options; that was their only style of reading. After treatment, the SSS readers can actually choose to read words the "normal" way. They can read whole paragraphs, whole books, if they want. They gain the capability of truly reading, even reading for pleasure, reading as much of the book as they wish. They no longer have to be limited to getting the minimal amount of required information.

As one teacher said:

> *I constantly bought books. I would read a chapter or two and then put the book down. It hurt to read, it wasn't comfortable, and it was just too much work. Now that the colored filters have stopped the distortions, I'm reading all those books that I've collected over the years.*

5.

The Role of SSS in Learning Disabilities

Many children have trouble learning in a school setting, despite having normal or above-normal intelligence. They seem unable to reach their potential, even though they demonstrate the ability to learn. The problem of learning disabilities is often called "the invisible handicap." Learning disabilities are a cluster of different problems that every day confuse and frustrate millions of people around the world.

WHAT ARE LEARNING DISABILITIES?

Learning disabilities can be defined simply as problems in any aspect of learning. They involve problems in the individual's ability to process, store, or recall information. As a result, there is a discrepancy between the person's true potential and his or her actual performance in day-to-day activities.

Public Law 94-142, the Education for all Handicapped

Children Act of 1975, offers a definition: "Specific learning disability means a disorder in one or more of the basic psychological processes involved in understanding or in using language, spoken or written, which may manifest itself in an imperfect ability to listen, think, speak, read, write, spell, or to do mathematical calculations. The term includes such conditions as perceptual handicaps, brain injury, minimal brain dysfunction, dyslexia and developmental aphasia. The term does not include children who have learning problems that are primarily the result of visual, hearing or motor handicaps, of mental retardation, of emotional disturbance, or of environmental, cultural, or economic disadvantage."

Although learning disabilities encompass a variety of problems, many parents believe all academic difficulties are related. That is why they often look for one solution to what might be, in actuality, three or more distinct problems. But learning problems are complex, involving many different factors. Let's take the example of L.S., age 11. The child appears inattentive, distractible, and is not performing in class. It appears he is avoiding reading and writing. A more detailed analysis of L.S.'s school performance indicates he is having difficulty learning to memorize and retain spelling words; memorizing math facts is an almost impossible chore; writing is tiring and laborious; and he must take frequent breaks when reading and writing. Does it seem likely that any one treatment could help his reading, writing, spelling, and math deficits?

WHO EXPERIENCES LEARNING DISABILITIES?

Learning disabilities are, unfortunately, fairly common. Current government figures from the United States, Great Britain, and other countries estimate that approximately 10 percent of the general population has some type of learning disability. Those disabilities are more noticeable in children. Why? By the time children become adults, they have often developed compensatory strategies to deal with their problems. Also, by then there is less of an ongoing need for reading and other academic activities as there might be while in school. The United States Department of Education estimates that there are at least 2 million children who are learning disabled in America today. More than one of every seven public school students might need special education services. At least half of those probably have some type of learning disability. Many more people, who have not been labeled as learning disabled, are recognized as not living up to their potential in school, work, or other settings; the cause of the unfulfilled potential is often not understood.

SOME OF THE PROBLEMS

Children with learning disabilities might have any or all of these problems: difficulty reading, only being able to read portions of paragraphs, skipping words, reversing or changing the order of letters in a word, unable to tell right from left, trouble recognizing words on paper, problems listening, problems telling time, and a short attention span. There might be problems in concentration, perception, visual and auditory processing, skills linking perception to movement, orientation in time and space, short- or long-term memory, language skills, and abstract reasoning.

Children with learning disabilities exhibit a great variability in their performance from task to task or in the way they handle the same task from day to day. They excel at some activities and fail miserably at others. Often, skills that seem solid one day are gone the next. It is that inconsistency, the uneven, high-low pattern of their performance, that confuses teachers and parents.

Each person is affected differently. Some children are disorganized, work very slowly, rarely finish assignments, and seem confused much of the time. They have trouble organizing skills into a coherent and useful whole.

Because of learning disabilities, some children might become easily frustrated and lose interest in schoolwork. Their self-image might decrease dramatically, and they often become angry and frustrated. They might behave badly and aggressively. Many children with learning disabilities show symptoms of inattentiveness, impulsiveness, and hyperactivity.

Individuals with learning disabilities might have trouble handling day-to-day activities, even if they have average or above-average intelligence. Some individuals with learning disabilities are even gifted.

Many learning-disabled children grow up to become adults with the same academic difficulties. Many eventually seek help in learning disability programs in colleges or universities.

HOW THE LEARNING DISABLED SEE THEMSELVES

Dumb, stupid, and lazy are the three most common terms the learning disabled use to describe themselves. They spend a lifetime sitting in the classroom, where everyone else is able to read five pages while they are struggling to get through one. They do not need anyone to tell them they are not successful. All they have to do is look around them to confirm how "dumb" they are.

WHERE LEARNING DISABILITIES COME FROM

The causes of learning disabilities are still in question. Learning disabilities might stem from more than one underlying abnormality.

Sometimes, learning disabilities exist in other members of the same family, suggesting a hereditary factor.

In some, the learning disability comes from an injury to the nervous system, perhaps caused at birth or from high fevers or a concussion. Sometimes it is explained as developmental delays or maturational lags, and parents are told their child will outgrow the problem.

Some theories suggest that children who have learning disabilities have problems with the way the brain handles information. There might be a malfunction in the brain, but no conclusions have yet been formed about how or why the malfunction occurs. There might be nothing wrong with those children's ability to obtain information. In other words, their five senses might be fine, but the problem occurs in the brain after the information has been received. Researchers are also exploring the effects of biochemical and nutritional imbalances on the brain and its development.

Learning disabilities might also occur as a result of other factors, including abnormally low birth weight, infections of the central nervous system, brain damage from infection, fetal alcohol syndrome, and severe head injury. The cause of learning disabilities is still in question. One thing we do know is that learning disabilities do not go away on their own.

TYPES OF LEARNING DISABILITIES

There are a number of categories of learning disabilities: visual perceptual, auditory perceptual, memory, motor problems, hyperactivity/distractibility, and dyslexia.

Visual Perceptual

Learning-disabled individuals in the visual perceptual category have difficulty with reading and writing activities.

They often are inattentive readers. Letters seen by the reader might be reversed, rotated, inverted, or confused with other letters or words. The reader might daydream while reading or have trouble beginning or completing assignments. Individuals might find it a problem to write, copy, spell, or keep numbers in columns. This group survives in school by listening, memorizing, and talking. Many of their problems can be related to SSS.

Auditory Perceptual

Some individuals have difficulty learning because they have trouble listening and picking up information auditorily. Taking notes might be a problem, and verbal information might be misinterpreted. More energy and effort must be put into listening. They might be more successful getting information from printed text than from what they hear. Both tuning out what is going on and daydreaming are not uncommon. This group might have trouble recalling or identifying sounds.

Memory

Individuals in this group might have trouble with spelling, math, reading, and learning activities requiring good memory skills. Retention problems might continue even after much practice and repetition with the desired information. Students in this group might have difficulty learning the alphabet, sight vocabulary, word spellings, and mathematical facts.

Motor Problems

Some people have difficulty copying from books or chalkboards, taking notes, spelling, or taking tests. They have problems with the actual process of writing. They might know the material, but by writing, they're actually translating it into another form. That might result in errors. Their handwriting might be sloppy or practically illegible, and they might unconsciously omit words. Their writing might be readable if they really try, but it gradually deteriorates. Writing is tiring and laborious.

Hyperactivity/Distractibility

Some people have trouble paying attention, concentrating, listening, and even sitting still. That can cause a lot of trouble in school. Students in this group are impulsive, easily distracted, tend to daydream a lot, and often are unable to complete their assignments. Environmental allergies, food allergies, attention deficit disorder, and Scotopic Sensitivity Syndrome are just a few of the factors that can cause a child to appear distractible or hyperactive. The more numerous the factors that contribute to inattention, the greater the difficulty in pinpointing and controlling the symptoms.

Dyslexia

Some individuals have difficulty processing sounds and letters. Spelling, reading, and writing are problems for them. (More about dyslexia can be found in the next chapter.)

ASSESSING LEARNING DISABILITIES

Learning disabilities are identifiable problems. A child who has one has been tested, and the results show a discrepancy between his or her potential and actual academic achievements. Specific guidelines vary, but a learning disability usually means that achievement is at least two grade levels below the expectancy. That is very arbitrary, though. If the discrepancy is great enough, the school identifies the child as having a specific learning disability and provides help, possibly in the form of a special program for part of the day or special classes all day long.

It's important to diagnose learning disabilities as early as possible in the child's educational career. Although it is often difficult to determine if a child has a learning disability before he or she is six or seven years old, the sooner it is detected the better. That way, the child can receive special services and treatment sooner. Learning disabilities that are not diagnosed until later often become more severe as the school curriculum becomes more complicated. That can make it even more difficult for the child.

Federal laws require schools to evaluate any child who is suspected of having a learning disability or who simply is not functioning well in school. Those evaluations, which are at no cost to parents, typically include consultations with medical doctors, psychologists, and educators to determine what problems exist and whether physical or psychological factors are the cause.

WHAT PARENTS CAN LOOK FOR

Symptoms of learning disabilities to watch for include delays in language development, problems with speech, difficulties with coordination, and a short attention span. Children who have learning disabilities might have difficulty understanding what they see or hear. But remember, the existence of any of those symptoms does not necessarily mean the child has a learning disability. Parents who have questions or concerns about their child's development should speak to the child's physician or an education expert.

What else can parents look for? Watch for any child who is putting more energy into the learning process than normally would appear necessary. Parents need to be sensitive to how many and how often compensatory strategies are used to survive in the classroom.

Parents might ask, "Do I read assignments to my child? Do I edit my child's work before it is turned in? Must I work alongside my child for work to be completed? Does it take my child hours to complete simple homework assignments? Does my child have difficulty putting ideas down on paper? Does my child resist doing written work? Does my child dictate his work and then copy what I have written down?"

HOW SSS IS INVOLVED

Scotopic Sensitivity Syndrome is not, in and of itself, a learning disability. However, research has indicated that almost half of those who have been diagnosed as having a learning disability have Scotopic Sensitivity Syndrome as one component of their learning problem.

If an individual with a learning disability has SSS, it can affect his or her reading, spelling, math, and writing; it can spur distractibility, hyperactivity, and other things. The individual might miss words when copying from a chalkboard or a book, might make math errors because of an inability to keep numbers in columns, and might make sloppy errors because of difficulty keeping writing on the line or drawing letters of an equal size. Sometimes, writing is too close together; or it can be too large, with unequal spacing. A child's trouble sitting still or completing or even beginning reading or writing assignments might be because of SSS.

Reduced reading ability, more reading errors, and poor comprehension might result from SSS. Usually, the degree of the perceptual distortions is more severe for those with both SSS and learning disabilities than for the typical student who has SSS only. Instead of words moving slightly, they might shift significantly or swim off the page. Instead of the page's giving the reader mild discomfort, the white background might form patterns or obliterate parts of letters, punctuation marks, or even whole words.

Difficulties with spatial orientation, penmanship, reading, spelling, math, hyperactivity, attention, and certain fine and gross motor skills might be partially or wholly due to SSS.

ASSESSMENT DIFFICULTIES

Standardized tests are used to determine whether someone has learning disabilities. The tests measure very specific aspects of learning, but they also suggest that those are the only elements that constitute a learning disability. Because of that, people who are scotopic might not be identified at all as having a problem. Or they might be labeled as learning disabled, but for a different reason. A person might have more than one reason or problem contributing to a learning disability, and the standardized tests might identify certain factors but not Scotopic Sensitivity Syndrome.

PROBLEM WITH MISDIAGNOSIS

Children who have undiagnosed SSS might remain in the special education system for years, at great expense to the district. It's not unusual for people diagnosed as learning disabled to be having problems with SSS. They might be placed in a resource room with a resource teacher or in a self-contained classroom or, in some rare cases, be misdiagnosed as mentally retarded. They are then remediated based on the results of standardized tests. They can make progress, but it probably will be limited. Usually, no matter how much energy or effort is put in, no matter how much the curriculum is modified, no matter how many methods or modes for teaching are implemented, those children still seem to encounter obstacles to their learning. They still make inadequate progress or maybe don't move along at all.

It's as if something is holding up their learning. Nobody knows what that thing is, but every time you try to introduce a new way of teaching, some unknown factor blocks the way. So learning just doesn't progress, or it progresses only so far.

Remediation just continues to make the children feel stupid and lazy. It's as if you've skied for a long time but can't parallel ski and never understood why. You don't particularly enjoy skiing since it is such hard work, but you keep on trying. You look around when you ski and think that there must be something you can do. There must be a little trick, but you don't know it. You keep trying to find out what that trick is by watching others. Nothing works! You can't improve, so skiing remains a chore—tiring, frustrating, and exhausting.

That's what a lot of children do with reading. They can't understand what's holding them back. What's keeping them from flowing easily across the printed page? What's stopping it from coming automatically? They watch everyone else and say, "This person is bending over when they read so I'll try bending over when I read." Or, "I'll try mouthing the words when I read." Or, "I'll try using my finger when I read." Or, "There has got to be some little trick that will help it happen for me. Because everybody else can do it and I can't." Or, "Everyone always told me to just try harder and I could do better, but no one ever told me how!"

In skiing, a person can go down the slopes and watch everybody fly by and think, "Why can everyone else do it and I can't, unless there is something really wrong with me?"

In education, if professionals are unable to pick up those critical elements that are holding back the process, then students will be able to get only to a certain point and no further. That's what is happening to children who are diagnosed as learning disabled without the recognition that Scotopic Sensitivity Syndrome might be a critical element of their learning disability. That does not mean SSS is the only element; there can be many reasons why any child or adult is having problems learning.

THE LEARNING-DISABLED STUDENT WITH SSS

Imagine this scenario: The special education class is busy reading an assignment. The teacher instructs the students to stop reading, number an answer sheet, and respond to questions that have been written on the blackboard. The requests appear reasonable, but one girl silently struggles. She is a learning-disabled student who has SSS. She has been able to complete only a small portion of the reading assignment because the words keep changing, and the longer she tries the more distorted becomes the print. She is unable to stay on the right lines or to make sense out of the assortment of spots that swirl before her eyes.

She is unsuccessful at reading the questions on the chalkboard because, even though she knows the words, they seem to melt into the background. Everytime she looks away to write a letter on her page she cannot find her place on the chalkboard again. The harder she tries, the worse she feels. The more anxious she gets, the more mistakes she makes. She painstakingly puts the numbers between shimmering lines on the paper. Sometimes the numbers get in the wrong spaces, so she gets the answers wrong even though she has the information. The modified instruction in the special education class allows the surrounding students to complete each task easily, leaving her—and any other learning-disabled children with SSS in the class—feeling inadequate.

A terrible feeling settles in the pit of her stomach at the beginning of the school day. By the end of the day, it has become a steel ball because of the endless hours of humiliation. She must read the assignments just like everyone else. Because once in a while she is able to read words, they expect her to be able to do it all the time. But the expectations and demands are unrealistic. The reality is frustration, anxiety, panic, fear, and confusion. The classroom experience is a continual confirmation of feelings of inadequacy.

Scotopic learning-disabled students spend five days a week for a minimum of five hours a day feeling inadequate. The extra energy they put forth is never acknowledged. To others, it appears that they daydream and do not try hard enough. They are humiliated in front of the class, and their work is torn up. They must redo assignments repeatedly, but it is still not good enough. They never seem able to duplicate tomorrow what they have learned today. Other children pick on them and make fun of them. Worst of all is having to read aloud. The palms start to sweat, and the stomach starts to churn.

Because of put-downs, low grades, criticism, lack of praise, lack of support, and lack of recognition, learning-disabled children with SSS might become hostile.

No one ever praised what I did right. They only commented on what I did wrong.

They might carry anger with them for the rest of their lives. They might distrust the world, never believing anyone would understand or support them. The lack of trust can sometimes lead to manipulative and passive behavior. They might arrive late for appointments, not show up at all and falsely claim to have forgotten, or purposely incite authority figures. If they can get others mad at them, it will support their basic belief that people always treat them badly, allowing them to continue to distrust the world. Their anger at the system and the world is very real and dominates their lives because everything is harder to do when you are learning disabled, especially if SSS is an unidentified part of the problem.

If SSS is present but undetected, then no one is aware of the real reason that learning is so hard and progress is blocked. The learning-disabled students with SSS helplessly sit by as teachers tear up the results of intense effort and call it trash. Other children play on the schoolyard, while learning-disabled students with SSS struggle to complete assignments satisfactorily. Every day the cycle is repeated, further discouraging those children, who seem to everyone else to be making only a marginal effort.

The parents and teachers are unaware of what is holding back learning. They are unaware of the amount of effort and energy being applied to schoolwork. The sense of failure and discouragement is further reinforced by low grades, cruel and constant comments by other children, lack of support or praise from parents, and teachers' harsh evaluations of the child's efforts. Even sympathetic parents who try to supplement classroom activities at home unwittingly perpetuate feelings of failure and frustration.

TREATMENT

Remember that even when SSS is eliminated, all other problems don't just go away. Educational interventions, though, can be more effective at that point since, for some, a major factor no longer interferes.

Experts feel that the best treatment for learning disabilities is a multisensory approach. School districts are mandated by federal law to provide special programs for handicapped children, including those with learning disabilities. Sometimes, school districts are reluctant to test students suspected of having learning disabilities, because of the added expense, the subtlety of the disorder, or the educator's ignorance.

Typical treatment for learning disabilities includes assistance from trained teachers, reading specialists, or tutors to provide training in those areas where the child is weak. Those working with the child need to understand the difficulties the child is facing and must provide emotional support as well as academic services. Support personnel should also indicate ways the child can experience success in nonacademic activities.

Parental love and support are a very important part of treatment for learning disabilities. Some children might benefit from counseling and behavioral therapies.

When a single cause is believed responsible for a child's learning problems, the success or failure of treatment is judged by the overall change in school performance. Not only is that an inaccurate measurement, but it leads to many appropriate techniques' being thrown out because their results are not what is desired. Grades might not improve, treatment might not result in a cure, and problems might persist.

But there could be many contributing factors. Professionals and parents always search for the simplest solution, wanting one answer that will solve all the problems. Yes, it would be great if one technique could treat all skill deficits and improve school performance. But it doesn't usually work that way!

A child who has been chronically unsuccessful in

school will not necessarily show an immediate and consistent improvement in behavior as soon as any one deficit is correctly diagnosed and treated. Many factors and fears can still interfere with successful remediation of deficits and can keep all involved from seeing immediate improvement.

Improvement for those individuals occurs erratically. There will probably be frequent failures along the way to eventual success. The child might not be sure that success is actually achievable. The child might be more comfortable with failure and see it as a more predictable, less threatening phenomenon.

SLOW CHANGES

Often the progress from failure to success is slow, typically taking three years. The first year is a time to try out new skills and then revert to the safety of failure. For every improved grade, there is a slide back to poorer grades. It might seem that the student is not making progress and that the treatments are not working.

By the second year, successes usually are more consistent, with regressions less common. But it is not until the third year that new feelings of self-worth become fully integrated and academic success becomes consistent. But because the change takes so long and is so gradual, it is difficult to judge the effectiveness of any particular educational intervention.

6.

The Role of SSS in Dyslexia

"Growing up a Hemingway and not being able to read is a pretty terrible thing. Being dyslexic, I was afraid of reading scripts and memorizing. With my colored filters the words stop moving around the page, and I now read fast and furious."

—Margaux Hemingway, from an interview on the Sally Jessy Raphael television show, April 11, 1990.

D yslexia is a condition that makes reading, writing, spelling, and, in some cases, even speaking difficult for millions of people. Dyslexia is usually thought of as seeing letters in words switch around, but it can include many different problems. Dyslexia makes it difficult for individuals to learn information, to retain it, and to communicate it.

The word dyslexia is made up of two parts. "Dys" means something that is poor or inadequate. "Lexia" refers to verbal language. Putting it together, dyslexia refers to language difficulties.

WHAT IS DYSLEXIA?

There are a number of opinions about what dyslexia actually is. To the lay person, dyslexia simply means not being able to read. The dyslexic is not successful at making progress in reading, and there's little explanation as to why. No one seems able to determine a reason for it or to figure out how to change that pattern or ease the situation.

Most educators consider dyslexia a subtopic of the general category of learning disabilities, although many people choose (not always correctly) to use the terms interchangeably. The terms might seem interchangeable, especially when you notice the similarities in symptoms described in this chapter and the previous one. But there are major differences.

Dyslexia affects social skills as well as academic ones. A dyslexic has limitations that are known but permanent. With other learning disabilities, if the educational system can correctly identify the problem and program the right type of remediation, it eventually will be able to mainstream the child back into the regular classroom.

Dyslexia is much more complex than, for example, simply having difficulty understanding words. Dyslexia might not affect all components of language function. An individual might have trouble reading words in one place but will read those same words correctly in another place.

The World Federation of Neurology defines dyslexia as "a disorder manifested by difficulty in learning to read despite conventional instruction, adequate intelligence, and sociocultural opportunity. It is dependent upon fundamental cognitive disabilities which are frequently of constitutional origin."

It is probably just as important to mention what dyslexia is not. Dyslexia is not a type of mental retardation. It is not an illness. It is not an indication that a person is incapable of learning.

Dyslexia, as with SSS and learning disabilities, can occur on a continuum. Although you might think otherwise, a dyslexic's intelligence is no different than anyone else's. Many are considered to have superior intelligence but are not succeeding, despite educational intervention.

WHAT DYSLEXIA DOES

Dyslexia opens the door to a range of symptoms and conditions. They can occur in different combinations and to various degrees of intensity.

The most common problem resulting from dyslexia is difficulty in dealing with letters, symbols, or numbers. Visual processing problems, as well as auditory processing problems, might indicate dyslexia. Dyslexics might have difficulty following directions, telling time, or finding places without getting lost. They might have problems with memory, coordination, depth perception, and discerning left from right.

The main visual processing problem shows up as incorrect oral reading. The person might omit, distort, or add words. (Sounds like SSS, doesn't it?) Naturally, that might affect comprehension. One can't understand material that cannot be processed!

A dyslexic's learning difficulties can lead to emotional problems. Self-esteem might be low for dyslexics who don't see themselves as normal. Friendships and socialization skills might suffer, and failures in school might leave the dyslexic very concerned about his or her future.

CAUSES OF DYSLEXIA

Despite much research, nobody yet knows what causes dyslexia. Current research is focused on such possible causes as genetics, physiology, biochemistry, and structural changes in the brain. There are theories that something is wrong with the brain or that certain chemicals are missing. One of the more popular theories is that dyslexia is a structural defect in the brain which involves the central nervous system. There are many forms of dyslexia, and as yet there is no cure.

Brains of individuals with dyslexia have, in many studies, been seen to be different from those without it. In most people who have adequate language skills, language areas on the left side of the brain seem more developed than those on the right. However, in dyslexics, the two seem about equally developed. Experts believe that this results in a struggle between the left side and the right side of the brain with regard to language function. That struggle results in reading difficulty. The greater degree of right-brain development in people with dyslexia might explain why dyslexics often do so well in creative arts, sports, and other spatial-based activities.

Regardless of the specific cause of dyslexia, the difficulties that individuals have with reading, writing, learning, and speaking can be very, very difficult to deal with.

HOW SSS AFFECTS DYSLEXIA

In 1925, neurologist Samuel Orton suggested that dyslexia is a dysfunction in visual perception and visual memory and is characterized by a tendency to perceive letters and words in reverse. The Orton Dyslexia Society now believes dyslexia to be a consequence of a limited facility in using language to code other types of information.

Some theorists feel there are three categories of dyslexics: those with a visually based problem, those with an auditorily based problem, and those with a problem that stems from a combination of both visual and auditory causes. Scotopic Sensitivity Syndrome concentrates on people who have difficulties with visual perception.

Even good readers with SSS have problems with ease or efficiency of reading. But what happens when interference from the print or the background becomes so severe that letters, words, sentences, or paragraphs cannot be recognized or read? Many times, those individuals are labeled dyslexic.

Doris couldn't learn the alphabet in kindergarten and couldn't learn to read in school. She was labeled mentally retarded and placed in special classes. Finally, in high school, she was diagnosed as dyslexic and moved into regular classes where she sat, listened, and was unable to perform. At age 35 she was still a non-reader.

Asked to describe the printed page, she reported that she did not see letters on the page; no, instead she saw lots of little black ants rapidly running around. If she worked real hard, Doris reported, she could stop the movement, and some of the ants would become letters. Then she could read that word.

Doris was labeled dyslexic because of limited reading progress and difficulty on standardized tests for dyslexia. The unasked question was whether she has dyslexia, Scotopic Sensitivity Syndrome, or both.

The underlying reading difficulty of Doris and many other individuals diagnosed as dyslexic is actually Scotopic Sensitivity Syndrome. What is sad and frightening is that once labeled dyslexic they will continue to have severe reading difficulties unless they are examined for SSS.

HOW DYSLEXICS WITH SSS SEE

The symptoms of SSS are varied and can be experienced individually or in combination. There is no one set of symptoms indicative of dyslexia, but the distortions can be severe enough to cause excessive interruption to the print so that major portions of the page become illegible. For dyslexics with SSS, the distortions appear quite rapidly, usually within five to ten minutes, sometimes even on the first line being read.

Weak readers and those who do not enjoy reading nevertheless receive enough data from the page to process the information. Dyslexics with SSS, however, cannot read the words. An inefficient reader might find that the white background becomes puffy and more noticeable than the black letters, while the dyslexic with SSS could find that the white background swallows up whole words or even sentences. This white-out effect could occur with such frequency that reading would be impossible. It might look like this:

The thought that   is that   are   it become hard to   and be able to   said by the
author. Rea   and comprh   become a   treme   e f rt.
Re d   spends   most   filling   in   anks   ahd   ping
   to   gues   at the eam g of th aut . Eventually, it
b co   t   h of a   fort to co   ue.

The person who avoids reading for pleasure might find that his range of recognition is only three or four words, which causes his reading to be slow and halting. But when an individual finds his range to be only one or two letters, reading becomes impossible. A sentence for the SSS dyslexic might look like this:

    I   w   a n t y   o u t   o   s e   e h o
i   t   i   s f   o r s   o m o   n e
t   o r e a d t h e   p a g e .

Perceptual distortions can include only a slight movement of words, so reading the page is possible although irritating and tiring; but the movement is extreme when SSS is seen in conjunction with dyslexia. Words can jump, switch, swirl around, and jump off the page almost immediately. All reading efforts are directed toward perception. Dyslexics with SSS might be trying to read pages that look like some of the figures in Chapter Three or like Figure 6.1.

HOW TREATMENT FOR SSS AFFECTS DYSLEXIA

For Doris, the 35-year-old who tried to read scurrying ants, the use of colored filters allowed her to see letters. She had acquired some reading skills despite the severe limitations posed by her distorted perception. Colored filters improved her reading immediately so that she could function easily on a third-grade reading level. An insurmountable task had become manageable, and she was eager to relearn basic reading skills.

Martha was a college student who had all her textbooks taped. She was unable to read. Whenever she tried, the letters had three, four, sometimes five images. Sometimes it got so bad that she saw one part of the page with one eye and another part with the other eye. She tried covering one eye, but some words swayed back and forth while others swirled around.

Martha was dyslexic. She received services from Recordings for the Blind and Disabled Student Services. She was dependent on others to read to her and take notes for her. She needed to take her tests orally. When Martha had been in first grade, her mother had insisted that they work together every night for forty-five minutes on reading skills. That practice had continued until college, despite a lack of progress.

After Martha was tested and treated for SSS, she made immediate and dramatic progress. What became apparent with the use of colored filters was that Martha had acquired a large sight vocabulary and adequate read-

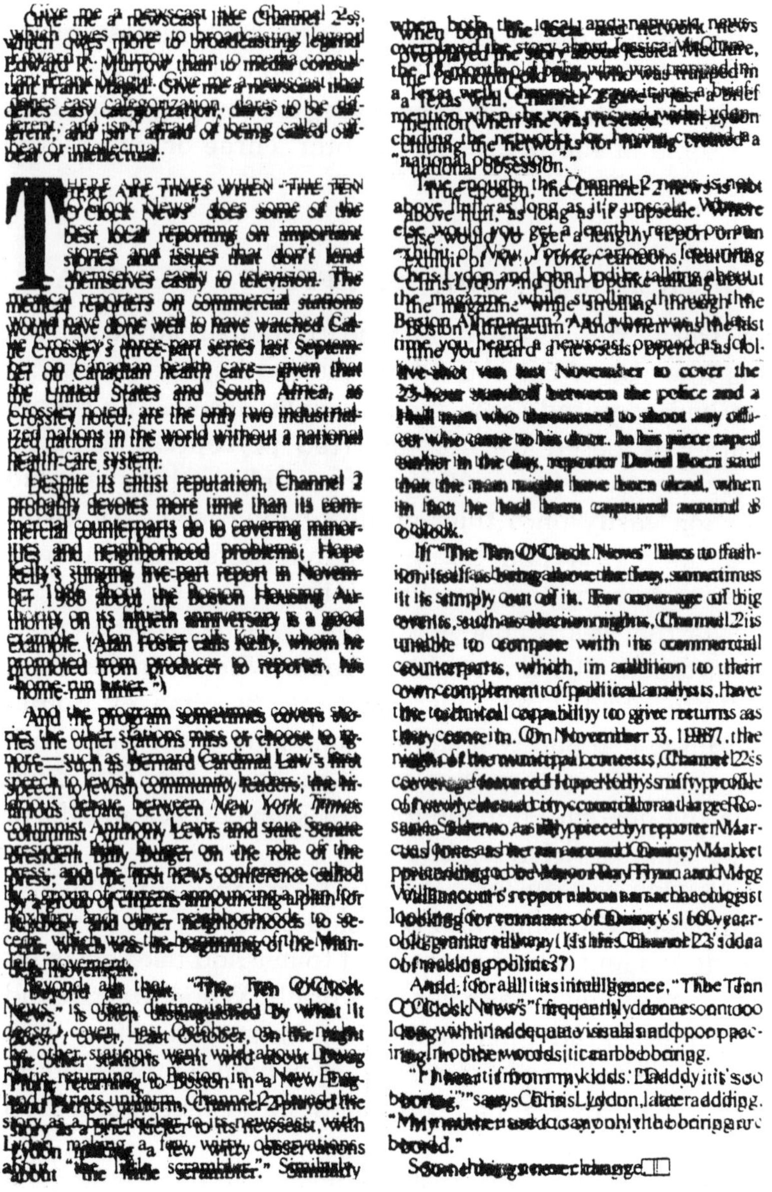
Give me a newscast like Channel 2's, which owes more to broadcasting legend Edward R. Murrow than to media consultant Frank Magid. Give me a newscast that defies easy categorization, dares to be different, and isn't afraid of being called offbeat or intellectual.

THERE ARE TIMES WHEN "THE TEN O'Clock News" does some of the best local reporting on important stories and issues that don't lend themselves easily to television. The medical reporters on commercial stations would have done well to have watched Cattie Crossley's three-part series last September on Canadian health care—given that the United States and South Africa, as Crossley noted, are the only two industrialized nations in the world without a national health-care system.

Despite its elitist reputation, Channel 2 probably devotes more time than its commercial counterparts do to covering minorities and neighborhood problems; Hope Kelly's stinging five-part report in November 1986 about the Boston Housing Authority on its fiftieth anniversary is a good example. (Alan Foster calls Kelly, whom he promoted from producer to reporter, his "home-run hitter.")

And the program sometimes covers stories the other stations miss or choose to ignore—such as Bernard Cardinal Law's first speech to Jewish community leaders; the hilarious debate between *New York Times* columnist Anthony Lewis and state Senate president Billy Bulger on the role of the press; and the first news conference called by a group of citizens announcing a plan for Roxbury and other neighborhoods to secede, which was the beginning of the Mandela movement.

Beyond all that, "The Ten O'Clock News" is often distinguished by what it *doesn't* cover. Last October, on the night the other stations went wild about Doug Flutie returning to Boston in a New England Patriots uniform, Channel 2 played the story as a brief kicker to its newscast, with Lydon making a few witty observations about "the little scrambler." Similarly when both the local and network news overplayed the story about Jessica McClure, the 18-month-old baby who was trapped in a Texas well, Channel 2 gave it just a brief mention when she was rescued, with Lydon chiding the networks for having created a "national obsession."

True enough, the Channel 2 news is not above it, as long as it's upscale. Where else would you get a lengthy report on an exhibit of *New Yorker* cartoons, featuring Chris Lydon and John Updike talking about the magazine while strolling through the Boston Athenaeum? And when was the last time you heard a newscast opened as fol-live-shot van last November to cover the 23-hour standoff between the police and a Hull man who threatened to shoot any officer who came to his door. In his piece taped earlier in the day, reporter David Boeri said that the man might have been dead, when in fact he had been captured around 8 o'clock.

If "The Ten O'Clock News" likes to fashion itself as being above the fray, sometimes it is simply out of it. For coverage of big events, such as election nights, Channel 2 is unable to compete with its commercial counterparts, which, in addition to their own complement of political analysts, have the technical capability to give returns as they come in. On November 3, 1987, the night of the municipal contests, Channel 2's coverage featured Hope Kelly's sniffy profile of newly elected city councilor at-large Rosaria Salerno as a lily piece by reporter Marcus Jones as the marquee Quincy Market preceding to the Mayor Ray Flynn and Meg Vaillancourt's report about an archeologist looking for remnants of Quincy's 160-year-old granite railway. (Is this Channel 2's idea of making politics?)

And, for all its intelligence, "The Ten O'Clock News" frequently does not do an adequate job on visuals and popping. In other words, it can be boring.

"I hear it from my kids: 'Daddy, it's so boring,'" says Chris Lydon, later adding, "My mother used to say only the boring are bored."

Something never change.

Figure 6.1. Dyslexia by itself is bad enough; so is SSS; but when the two are combined, the reader is faced with pages such as this.

ing skills through her intensive and lengthy remediation process but had been unable to use those skills. With the removal of the perceptual limitations, Martha was able to read at a college level. She no longer needed to have books read to her. She was able to function on her own.

The awareness that there is a connection between SSS and dyslexia has resulted in help for many individuals. Treatment for SSS is *not* a treatment for dyslexia. Treatment for SSS corrects an underlying visual perceptual problem. For some individuals, the correction leads to such improvement that they no longer need to be labeled dyslexic. But for dyslexics who have a multitude of problems, treatment for SSS eliminates only one of the layers that contributes to their dyslexia.

Some of the other problems many dyslexics have, such as distractibility, hyperactivity, poor directionality, and weak organizational and memory skills, will remain and require further attention. Unfortunately, those other problems might be so severe that no matter what treatment is given, the person would still have severe social or academic limitations.

Although Martha's reading improved dramatically, she still had difficulty with conceptualizing, memorizing, and retaining information. Changing her perception did not help her learn foreign languages or improve her ability to do math, especially algebra and calculus.

In some cases, even if SSS is identified and the perceptual difficulties are corrected, reading problems continue because of language and neurological-based difficulties. There can still be a major limiting effect on reading achievement.

For those dyslexics, even though they now can accurately perceive the page, they still have difficulty reading. Words still cannot be sounded out or read, even though they can be clearly and consistently perceived. That is because SSS does not affect encoding or decoding skills, so the use of colored filters cannot improve phonetics ability or increase a deficient sight vocabulary.

Carla has SSS but also has severe language problems that reduce her reading ability. Carla likes to wear her colored filters even though she still has to work at reading. Even though she gets frustrated at having to stop frequently to sound out words, she says that it no longer hurts to read and that she can keep at it longer.

REMEDIATION FOR DYSLEXIA

With the discovery of SSS and the use of colored filters, fewer individuals will be labeled dyslexic, and some already labeled might no longer be dyslexic. However, approximately one-third of diagnosed dyslexics will not benefit from SSS treatment. Their dyslexia has other causes, which are not understood; their problem is too complex for a clear-cut treatment.

It is accepted that dyslexia won't go away, won't change, and won't get better. Therefore, long-term multisensory remediation is required, and progress is limited. The person needs to accept the limitations of dyslexia and create strategies to deal with them.

COMPENSATORY STRATEGIES

For those with dyslexia, remediation and specialized education seldom lead to appropriate academic or social skills. To meet the impossible demands imposed by teachers, parents, and society, dyslexic students devise ingenious ways to get around the educational system and survive. Compensatory strategies allow individuals to function and achieve relative success despite a lack of basic skills.

Strategies are not the exclusive domain of individuals with dyslexia. Everyone periodically uses strategies, but dyslexics must use strategies on a daily basis. The average individual is neither aware nor concerned when using a strategy, but dyslexics who resort to strategies in the academic setting and in daily life feel as if any success they achieve has been attained by a form of cheating.

What about dyslexics who want to do well in school? How do they survive, especially when the educational system resists having textbooks read to them or giving them oral examinations?

Some students manage to get by without ever reading a book. They listen intently in class and respond often and appropriately during classroom discussions. Their teachers feel they have a good grasp of the information. They receive passing grades for courses even though they fail the tests, because they show a high interest and they try. As one high school student reported:

I fake it. I have a good personality, ask a lot of questions, pass a few tests, and fail most of them. The teachers feel sorry for me and pass me for trying.

Others manage to pass and even do well on tests without reading the assignments. They memorize lectures. They never miss class. They take classes with little required reading. Other students manage to pass tests by reading only parts of the assignments—the beginning of each paragraph and the summary at the end of each chapter.

Greg, a good student, used compensatory techniques to hide from his parents and teachers the fact that he couldn't read. He was successful until he took ill and missed three weeks of school. When he returned, he could not catch up.

Things became so bad that he had a nervous breakdown and was hospitalized.

Some students engage in avoidance behavior. They become involved in after-school activities that require travel and practice. Therefore, they get excused from some of the homework and tests. When that does not work, they fake being sick on test days.

Other techniques require the help of loved ones. Mothers, fathers, sisters, boyfriends, girlfriends, and others are enlisted to do everything from reading the assignments to writing reports. One student in college took all the same classes as her best friend so she could use that friend's notes. Others form study groups so they can learn the textbook material from discussions. One student obtained the reading lists ahead of time. Then he went out, purchased the books, and gave them to his mother. She would read them by herself and then discuss them with him. Although he knew the material, he always felt as if his mother, not he, had earned the degree.

Strategies to achieve without reading are useful outside the school setting, too, since dyslexics' problems are pervasive. Dyslexics use digital watches to tell time, ask for diagrams instead of written or oral directions, keep lists, tape-record instructions and lectures, and have others write down information for them.

So with compensatory strategies and hard work on the parts of all concerned, individuals with dyslexia can lead satisfying, productive lives.

IF LABELED DYSLEXIC, IS THAT ALL THERE IS?

With the discovery of SSS, professionals need to become sensitive to the fact that a person's being labeled dyslexic does not bar a partial or even total solution to the problem. If a case of dyslexia has SSS as one of its layers, then a partial answer is possible; and if a declared case of dyslexia is instead a mislabeled case of SSS, then a full solution might be reached.

It is important to understand the diverse rather than singular nature of dyslexia. People whose reading problems have many different etiologies are being diagnosed as dyslexic. It would be simplistic to assume that someone who is dyslexic has only SSS, attention deficit disorder, or some other neurological-based disorder. It might be damaging to stop searching for other answers. But even if treatment for Scotopic Sensitivity Syndrome does not cure dyslexia, just as it does not cure learning disabilities, it can still be one important element of the equation.

Ever since Kevin, a businessman in California, began reading, the words would turn yellow and green and even disappear. He saw words and phrases backward. Reading this sentence might have looked like this for him, and the longer he read the worse it became:

Gnidear hi sentence   might   ekil   dekool   evah this   him, and eht dear eh regnol the worse it   me.

> *I was given prescription lenses to read with, but they did nothing more than make words bigger and darker. I was given eye exercises. The tutor I had was more beneficial. She taught me study skills and organization techniques. But nothing helped my reading. I was diagnosed as dyslexic. I was told I just had to try harder.*
>
> *I was never able to read more than one chapter of any textbook. When taking tests I would become physically ill because of the movement of the words. Reading was never anything but a humiliating and exhausting experience.*
>
> *I saw a show on* 60 Minutes *called "Reading By the Colors." I found myself staring at the television with my mouth wide open in amazement. The de-*

scriptions given and the stories hit me hard. Not only were they describing me and what I went through growing up but, more importantly, for the first time someone was able to effectively explain my problems.

I called the dyslexia society after seeing the 60 Minutes show to find how to get help with colored lenses. They told me that this method could not help me. They said that the glasses may stop the written word from moving, but they won't help me learn. I became angry at these professionals who couldn't understand that if one cannot perceive the page correctly, the learning process will be impeded. These people were telling me that not being able to see the printed page had no impact on my dyslexia!

I have been wearing the lenses for a year and a half now. My reading skills have tripled. I can read for as long as I want without feeling sick. I have had to learn to process information much faster, as my reading speed has greatly increased.

In 1990, Erica, one of the reporters who worked on the *60 Minutes* story, told me her tale:

As a child I wore a watch, but I couldn't tell time. I couldn't distinguish my left from my right, so I did a lot of pointing. . . . It got to be a joke in the family whenever we took the car for a family outing. 'Go that way,' I would tell my parents. There were a lot of things I couldn't do. And it hurt, because I didn't know why.

In June of 1979, I finally got tested by the Orton Dyslexia Society. It seemed the obvious thing to do because Mom and Dad had heard that children who were considered exceptionally bright but were failing in school were classified as being dyslexic.

After fourteen hours of testing, the results con-firmed that I was developmentally dyslexic—what-ever that means. I was told then that I shouldn't expect too much of myself . . . I only had 'normal intelligence,' and chances of getting into a good school didn't look very promising.

In 1988, I found myself researching a story on the Irlen Institute. Its working title: Reading by the Colors. We've been told that story brought more phone calls than any other story aired on 60 Minutes . . . followed by a flood of letters . . . in-cluding a letter from the Orton Dyslexia Society telling us we were irresponsible in our reporting. To suggest that Helen Irlen could help dyslexics was cruel, because dyslexics couldn't be helped. I was outraged. To suggest that all learning-disabled chil-dren diagnosed dyslexic couldn't be helped was equally cruel. What was dyslexia anyway? And how come dyslexics couldn't be helped?

Eleven years ago, I was tested for dyslexia. I was told there were no remedies . . . no cures . . . just a word to explain why I had failed.

In March of 1990, I was tested again [at the Irlen Institute]. This time there were no excuses, no explanations, no words—just a pair of colored lenses to help me see why I didn't have to fail.

I still have dyslexia, but I no longer have to survive by only reading first, middle, and last chap-ters of everything. I can read it all!

7.

The Role of SSS in Other Related Problems

S SS can affect an individual in a number of ways that go beyond reading and learning difficulties. These related problems might not get suitably addressed, especially when professionals misdiagnose children because they don't even recognize what they're dealing with.

BEHAVIOR

Many children who have reading or learning problems try to cover them up. They might hide their lack of ability by behaving in ways that are unacceptable in the school setting. The message they're conveying: "I'd rather be bad than appear to be stupid."

What kinds of inappropriate behavior might be seen? Children in this category might appear defiant, act out against authority, or throw temper tantrums. They might be destructive or verbally or physically aggressive. They might lie or steal or display other antisocial, delinquent behavior.

As you can imagine, children who participate in those types of antisocial behavior will probably not be labeled as having a reading or learning problem! Instead, they might be labeled as antisocial or poorly motivated or as having behavioral or emotional problems.

Boys seem to have more of a tendency to act up. In class they might call attention to themselves, look like they are refusing to do work, try anything rather than say, "I can't do it." They'll slam books down. They'll cause a disturbance. They're more likely to have letters sent home because it looks like they are not trying.

They learn how to get out of a classroom quickly if they're going to be called on to read. It can feel better to get sent to the principal's office than to stand up in front of your own peers and make an absolute fool of yourself because you can't read! So, given a choice, children sometimes feel it's better to act up.

I learned to disrupt the class, sometimes with humor and often by talking back to the teacher. I'd say something funny or disrespectful, everyone would laugh, and it gave me the chance to get out of doing work. My teacher said I had antisocial behavior, and I was branded an unsatisfactory citizen.

Have you ever seen a child who truly doesn't want to learn? A child who chooses to sit in the classroom, five days a week, and misbehave? It rarely happens. There is usually another reason.

ATTITUDE

In terms of attitude, it's hard if you can't consistently meet the expectations of your teachers. It's hard to feel positive about yourself and school.

It's not unusual for children who have undiagnosed SSS and are unable to meet those expectations to start having attitude problems or to start not liking themselves. In many instances, teachers' expectations are so inappropriate for children with SSS that they start cutting classes and not showing up at school. Sometimes they drop out very early. Instead of working, they might daydream or even choose to become the class clown. They can't do what people ask them to do, and they don't know enough to say, "I can't do it." Such a child knows that everybody around him is able to do it but that he can't. So everyone else is fine, and he's a stupid, lazy, or bad person.

MOTIVATION

A lot of times, what looks like attitude and behavioral problems is the child's way of protecting himself or herself. Boys and girls do it very differently. Girls do more adaptive behaviors; boys do more maladaptive ones.

For example, if a girl in school is having difficulty completing assignments or reading and doesn't want anyone to know about it, she's probably going to use her social or verbal skills to get by in class. She'll try to talk her way through class. She might be kind to the teacher. She might do extra projects. She, by her own behavior, attempts to let the teacher know she's trying as hard as she possibly can. But the teacher sees a child who is not motivated to complete assignments or do well on tests.

By the time I was in the fourth grade, I knew I couldn't read, although sometimes I seemed very smart in class. I would listen carefully to what other kids were saying about the homework assignments or to the discussion in class, and then I would simply try to remember every detail that I had heard.

When we were told to read something in class, I would start reading with everyone else and then watch to see when they would turn the pages. I would skip ahead and read the last few paragraphs, then I would just make sure to turn pages at about the same time as everyone else. Just by doing that, I could always eagerly raise my hand to answer questions about the beginning of the assignment or about the end of the assignment.

At night, while trying to do my homework, I would call my friends and ask them questions to try to get as much information about the assignment as possible without actually having to read the text-book.

It wasn't because I was lazy or irresponsible, although my parents and teachers constantly told me that I could do better if I would just be willing to work harder. They didn't realize how hard I was actually working already. Late at night, I would be under the covers with a flashlight, trying to finish the reading assignments that were due the next day. I would look at the page, and the words seemed to shimmer and move.

All I could remember was how stupid I was and how hopeless it was for me to try to function at school. It didn't occur to me that I could become a success at anything I tried. I was so used to failure, to ridicule, to the assumption by those around me that I was not willing to succeed.

So it's not that children are not motivated to learn. Rather, the children aren't capable of doing it and don't understand what's holding them back. They are unable to tell the adults or the experts what is happening to them. They don't know what reading should be like. They don't understand why they can't do it and why everyone else can.

SELF-ESTEEM

Starting at a very young age, usually by first grade, children are very aware of what they are capable of doing and not capable of doing. They are very aware when the teacher says, "Let's read aloud," that other kids can easily do it and they can't.

They're aware that other children can finish the classroom assignments and that they're still only halfway through (if that far). With those kinds of realizations, they start internalizing bad feelings and statements about themselves. Rather than let the world know how dumb they feel they are, they hide their problems and feelings.

> *I had almost no recognizable self-esteem. I felt like a successful con artist. I had managed to fool a majority of the people around me into thinking I was smart. I had even risked returning to college. In looking back, I desperately wanted my teachers to recognize the real me, not the slow, unresponsive student they saw on a daily basis. I always felt that my inability to read was [caused by] my lack of self-discipline or diligence.*

Some students with SSS and reading problems are never identified, because they get passing grades and work hard. It is assumed that is the very best they can do. There seems to be no real indication that the person has a problem.

Even though those children get passing grades, they know they could do better. They feel they are as bright and capable as their friends who are getting A's. Whatever the problem is, it's unidentified. The parents and school feel that those children are doing as well as they can. They are working up to their potential. But the real question is how much better they can do once SSS is identified and corrected.

What about the gifted students with SSS? Those children do not fit into the gifted classes, because of their reading difficulties; and they are too bright, with excellent coping strategies, to benefit from specialized learning disability services. Talk about not fitting in! Help from specialized classes might be harder to get, but the students are bright, and many times by working extra hard they can cover up their reading failure. Still, it could be so much easier for those children if they were tested for SSS.

DEPTH PERCEPTION

Some people with SSS have difficulty with depth perception. SSS is a perceptual problem that, in some cases, leads to difficulties in judging distances and spatial relationships. That can affect a number of very specific areas in life. Driving, for example, can be a problem. People with SSS might have difficulty judging their distance from curbs and parked cars. If the other cars are moving, that judgment can be even more difficult. SSS can affect their ability to do certain simple things, like changing lanes, because they're not really sure where the other cars are. Is there one right next to them? Do they have enough room? It might affect their ability to make turns across oncoming traffic. They might decide to wait until there's no traffic around them rather than turn and possibly hit someone.

Some people with SSS perceive everything as slightly farther away than where those things are in reality. So they think they have more room in which to maneuver. They walk around and think they have clearance, but they keep bumping into tables, doors, or walls.

Some people with SSS have trouble seeing things in three dimensions. The world has a "picture book" effect;

it's all in two dimensions. For example, they really can't tell that a tree is round. Their experience tells them it's round; when they feel it, they know it's round; but when they see it, it doesn't look round. They might see three trees that look like they're stacked one on top of another but in reality are not. There might even be a street in between each of those trees. The world takes on a kind of flat, painted perspective for them.

Someone with SSS might have difficulty picking objects up and putting them down. They might not be sure when to release an object when placing it down, and when they let go it falls on the table. They might try to pick up a glass, but instead they hit it. They might have been yelled at when growing up for spilling milk, knocking things over, being clumsy. Clumsy is a word that's used a lot with this group; they actually look clumsy.

Simple carpentry tasks become major projects. Sawing a straight line or hammering without hitting fingers becomes close to impossible.

> *I always felt like an accident waiting to happen. I told people I couldn't cook, because I couldn't safely cut or chop with sharp knives. My depth perception was so distorted, to do so would be to risk amputation of my finger tips, and my fingers were something I wanted to keep around.*

SPORTS

SSS can affect people athletically. Playing ball might be unbelievably difficult. In baseball, catching a fly ball can be virtually impossible for those with SSS because it would require them to look at the ball, judge its path, visually follow it, then reach out a hand with perfect timing and precision movement. Other sports might also be affected, including tennis, pingpong, and golf.

Persons with SSS might see more than one ball coming at them and have to guess which one is real. If they reach for the wrong one, the real one can hit them in the face! Then Dad, who's a super athlete, keeps thinking that with practice it will all come together! So individuals with SSS eventually become terrified, because they don't know how to stop from getting hit in the face. It is easier to avoid ball sports and similar activities than to do them poorly.

JUDGING MOVEMENT

Certain activities involving moving objects other than cars can also be difficult. For example, getting on and off escalators can present a problem. Escalators are moving, and the person with SSS might have trouble accurately judging when to step on and off. That can be very traumatic. They'll start figuring out how to compensate, or they'll even avoid using escalators!

With stairs, they might find it hard to judge depth. They might not be sure where to put their feet. When they put a foot down, it might not be onto a stair but just into the air. It's hard to judge accurately where a stair ends.

ENVIRONMENT

Just as not everyone sees the printed page the same way, not everyone has the same perception of their environment. Some people see things around them in bits and pieces. It's difficult for them to form an actual image of their surroundings. Rather than seeing or being able to visualize a complete picture, whether it is of an elephant, a house, a person, or an area, only one part of the picture is seen at a time. Therefore, those with SSS might not have a detailed image of objects, people, or spatial organization. Their whole picture might be broken into scattered fragments, like a jigsaw puzzle, but with no cohesive organization or composition.

> *I couldn't recognize friends unless they were up close. If I looked directly at someone's face, the middle of their face would just disappear. Or I'd see two or three noses moving around or parts of faces.*

COORDINATION

SSS can affect a person's coordinated movement and activity. For example, think of a child unleashed in a small playground. Have you ever seen the little merry-go-rounds that spin around when pushed? Children jump on and off. Children with SSS can't do that. They have to wait until it stops before they're able to get on and off. If they are climbing on "monkey bars," they have to look very carefully where they're going to put their hands. Jumping rope is very difficult. You have to be able to tell where the rope is and then be able to move accurately to get in and out.

MUSIC

Distortions that appear on the printed page can be magnified if you're reading music. Music is written out as a lot of tiny dots on or between many lines. Not only do you have dots identifying the notes, but you have symbols telling you how loudly or softly to play. Many people with SSS find that they can't tell which line a note is on, and some think the notes are supposed to move in time to the music! The lines might wave or cross, and the notes might appear and disappear, making the music very difficult to read.

> *During my piano lessons I never looked at the notes. I stared at the teacher's hands and memo-*

*rized the placement of the hands. When I went
home, I practiced, but I never looked at the notes.
I stared at my own hands and remembered the
movement patterns.*

Another student said he had a good auditory memory
for the music. He memorized the pieces, went home, and
played them again and again until he had them learned.
No one ever found out that he couldn't read music. Many
people with SSS compensate by memorizing physical
movements or playing by ear.

MATH

SSS problems can occur in specific academic areas, such
as math. Math problems involve keeping numbers in columns, accurately reading numbers in columns, and putting the answers down in the correct columns. Columns of
numbers, especially if there are many columns tightly
packed together on a page, will result in far more distortions. There might be reversals in numbers, numbers
moving from side to side, or numbers disappearing. All of
that contributes to a difficult time in coming up with an
accurate answer!

Of course, it is possible that if you gave those children
a problem to do in their heads, without having to look at
numbers, they would have little difficulty. So they might
know how to add and subtract, they might know the
concepts, and they might even have their facts memorized. They can come up with the right answer.

But given a problem on paper, math students with SSS
can appear sloppy. They might transpose number se-
quences. They might have difficulty tracking down columns because they mingle numbers from neighboring columns. They might be unable to place numbers consistently in correct columns to solve problems. Many

students compensate by constantly rechecking, which slows down their work rate.

HANDWRITING

Handwriting is another activity affected by SSS. Students might have trouble writing on the line, drifting either above it or below it. Some might have handwriting characterized by letters bunched together too closely or spread too far apart. Letters might have incorrect size relationships or connections. (See Figures 7.1, 7.2, and 7.3.)

WRITING

In addition to difficulties with handwriting, written expression can suffer. Those students might not consistently see punctuation when reading. Consequently, punctuation rules are taught in isolation without being reinforced by their reading experiences. Students therefore might have difficulty correctly applying rules of punctuation and grammar to writing. Their punctuation marks might tend to be scattered, random, or omitted altogether. Their essays often lack organization since they often write without rereading. Why add to the torture? It's hard enough for them to read while they are writing, but it's even more painful to have to go back and reread to make sure their work says what they want it to say.

COPYING

Copying from a chalkboard or from a book is also a difficult task. It's hard for them to keep going back and finding their place after they look away to copy, since characters might not be there when they look back.

Copying becomes a struggle that requires great concentration; words, letters, or numbers can bounce around

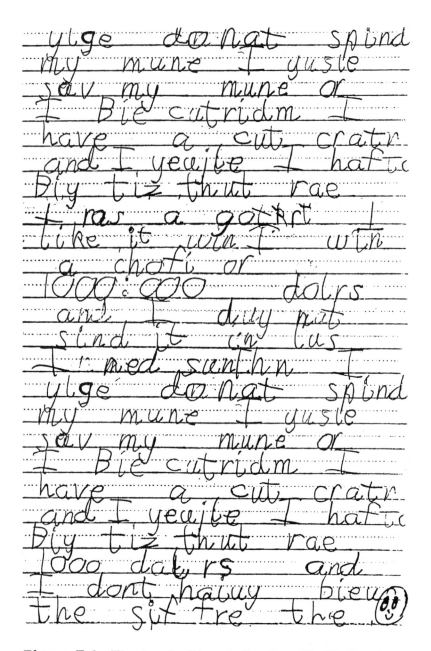

Figure 7.1. The handwriting of Jonathan R. Hitchcock on September 19, 1990, before he was fitted with filters.

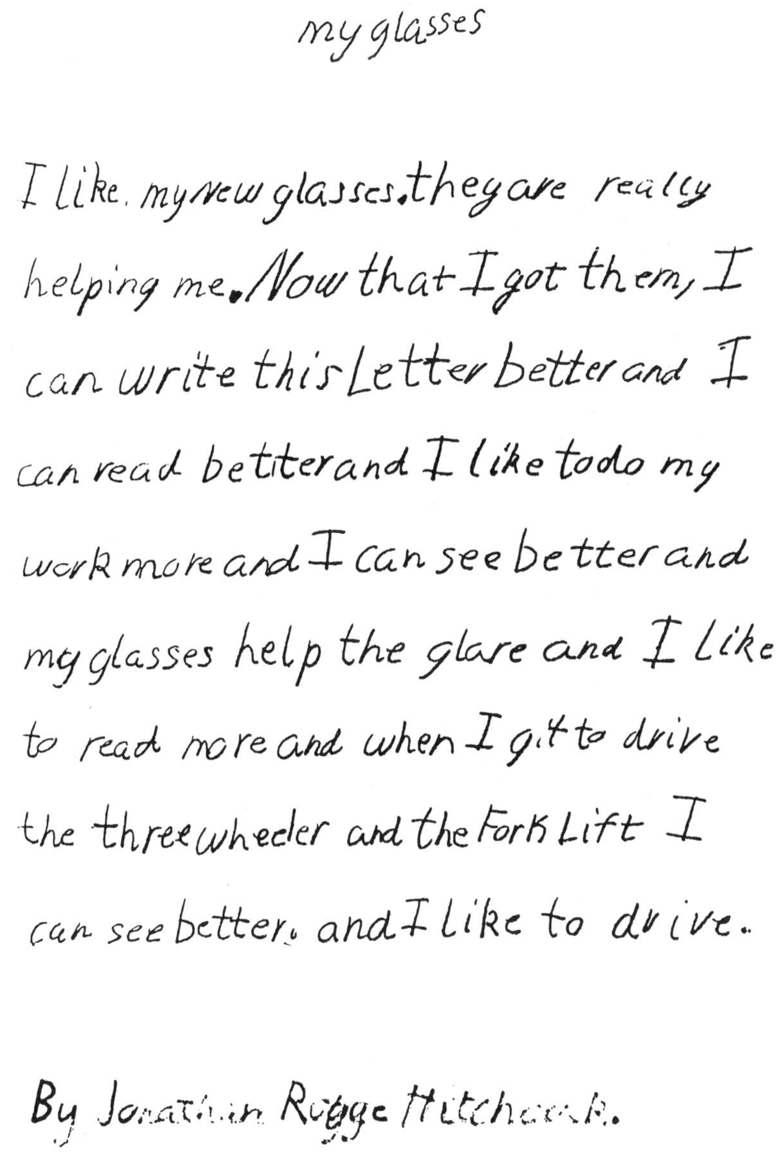

my glasses

I like my new glasses. they are really helping me. Now that I got them, I can write this Letter better and I can read better and I like to do my work more and I can see better and my glasses help the glare and I like to read more and when I git to drive the three wheeler and the Fork Lift I can see better. and I like to drive.

By Jonathan Rugge Hitchcock.

Figure 7.2. Hitchcock's writing on November 19, 1990. During the two-month interim, the 8-year-old boy was fitted with filters.

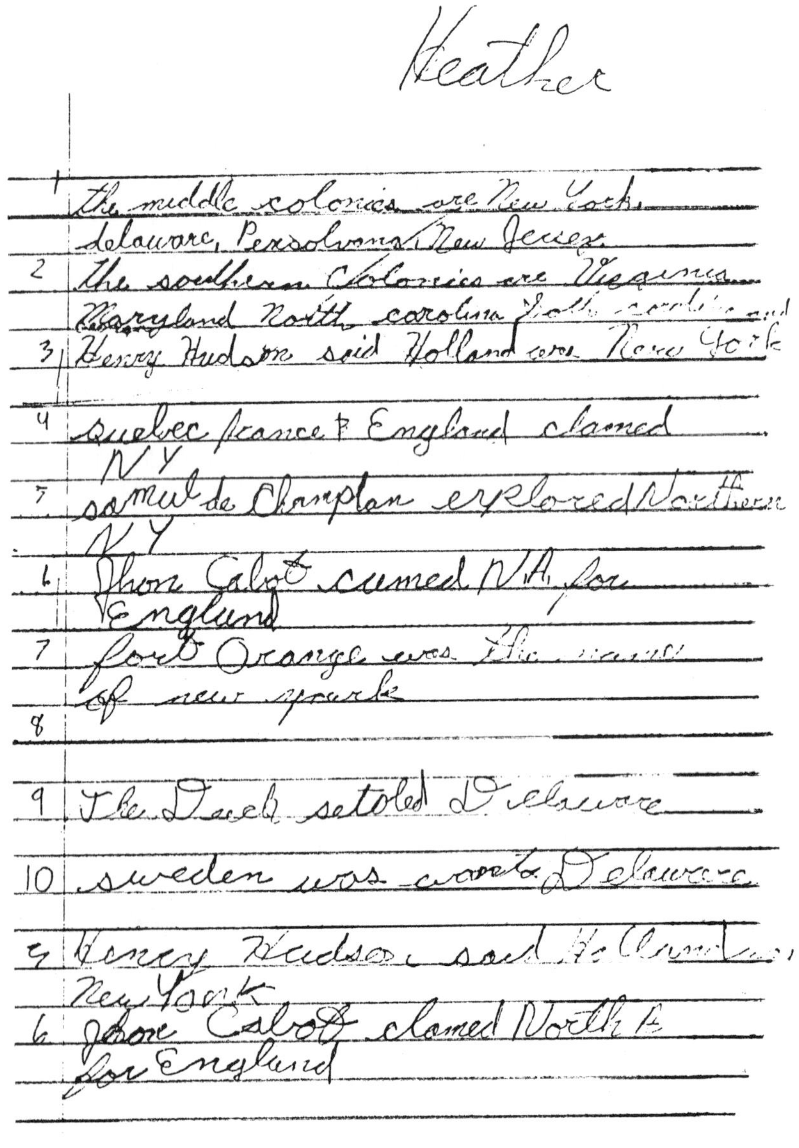

Heather

1. the middle colonies are New York, delaware, Pensolvana, New Jersey
2. the southern Colonies are Virginia Maryland North carolina South carolina and
3. Henry Hudson said Holland was New York
4. Quebec france & England clamed NY
5. samul de Champlan explored Northern NY
6. John Calbot cumed NA for England
7. fort Orange was the name of new york
8.
9. The Duch setoled Delaware
10. sweden was crossed Delaware
5. Henry Hudson said Holland New York
6. John Calbot clamed North A for England

Figure 7.3. Letters keep drifting from the baseline in this school assignment by a scotopic individual.

or drift away, or an individual might not perceive whole columns and rows. Those people cannot copy information without getting lost.

SSS can affect individuals in a number of ways, whether related to reading, academic areas, or other life situations. I'm sure you're beginning to get the idea. There are many academic areas, as well as related fields (such as art, typing, and computers) where SSS can have an impact. Let's not assume that all individuals who have any of those problems necessarily have SSS, but many of them probably do.

8.

Screening for SSS

Before anything can be done to treat Scotopic Sensitivity Syndrome, it must be identified. Although SSS has had such a devastating impact on reading and learning for thousands, if not millions, of individuals, painfully few school districts, teachers, psychologists, or vision specialists are even aware that SSS is something to be investigated.

There are only a comparatively few experts or facilities able to screen properly for SSS. But let's learn about what those individuals who are referred for screening will experience.

REFERRALS FOR SSS SCREENING

Many individuals who come for screening are referred by another family member. Parents who have problems reading will probably know whether their child is struggling. How? They can see the child experiencing many of the same or similar problems as they themselves experience.

Those parents might have heard or read something about SSS and feel it might apply to them and possibly to their child. So they bring the child in for screening. Usually the child's problem is addressed first and, subsequently, when the parents see the benefits, they seek help for themselves. Parents often will say, "I wanted to wait and see what this did for my child. Now that I've seen how much my child has benefited, I'm willing to go for screening myself."

Parents do a good job of identifying potential problems in their children. Yes, there are times when parents don't want to think about it. But often, if their children are not doing well in school, they'll start looking carefully to see what is wrong. In many cases, parents can pick up potential problems as well as, if not better than, the schools can. But it matters less who picks up the problem. What's more important is that it gets picked up!

Another source of referrals is educators. They might notice that a child they're working with is not progressing properly, even with special help and instruction. They might be concerned that something else is holding back the reading and learning process.

A third source of referrals is health professionals. For example, parents often consult physicians if they have concerns about a problem with their children. They'll ask for suggestions as to who can best help them.

Referrals are also received from psychologists who, in the process of testing children who are having behavioral or emotional or other problems, are concerned that there might be underlying academic difficulties. And since one of those underlying problems could be Scotopic Sensitivity Syndrome, they might refer those children.

A large number of referrals come by word of mouth from people who have been identified as having SSS, have been treated, and have made progress with colored filters or overlays. They often are very proud of what they've accomplished. They'll talk to anyone who will listen.

SCREENING—THE FIRST STAGE

The process for overcoming SSS is divided into two stages: screening, which will be discussed in this chapter, and treatment, which will be discussed in the next chapter.

The purpose of screening is to determine who has SSS. Individuals tested are those whose academic progress, reading ability, or other activities might be affected by Scotopic Sensitivity Syndrome.

LAYER REMOVAL

A learning or reading problem can be presented as a concept of layers. There can be one layer or several to any problem. Dealing with the problem as a whole is usually unproductive. It's better to try to peel off the layers. SSS is just one layer for some people, just one piece of the puzzle.

The fact that SSS is one possible layer in the whole picture is very important. Parents often assume that if the child has a problem, there's only that one problem. They feel if they could identify that one problem, and more importantly find a solution to it, then all the child's academic or reading problems will go away. But that's not true. And it's especially not true in relation to SSS. Yes, there are a percentage of cases where SSS is the only problem. (If that's so, you can get dramatic changes quickly.) But more typically, a child's reading or learning problem might actually comprise two, three, or more different layers or pieces. All those pieces come together in the child who has academic difficulties and make it look as if there is just one problem: the child just can't learn.

It is usually very difficult to separate the various layers. SSS is the exception. With SSS it's simple, because you can easily identify the one particular component, treat it, and immediately eliminate it.

In education, you usually don't talk about removing a problem. In fact, if you do talk that way, the first reaction you'll often get is that your approach is a scam, because nothing in education may have a quick-fix solution. So anything that looks like a quick fix is looked at with great skepticism.

In education we usually deal with long-term methods, slow progress, and intensive kinds of remediation. If a child needs reading remediation or special education, it's not for a day or a week. The process usually requires a commitment for a long period of time, probably years.

Because SSS is one of the few problems in education—if not the only one—that can be quickly eliminated, much attention is being focused on it, and screening is so very important.

TESTING—BUT MISSING SSS

When diagnostic clinics evaluate children for possible learning problems, they might do psychological testing, an educational evaluation, a social history, and a complete medical history. In cases where it's necessary, they'll do a psychiatric evaluation.

When I asked some of the children and adults why, during those previous testing situations, they had never said anything about their problem, they answered, "Nobody ever asked us. Nobody ever asked us what happens on the page, whether words are jumping on the page, what goes on in the background, so why would we know enough to say anything?" Some children don't say anything for fear that people will get mad at them for having a problem. They want to be just like everyone else.

Unfortunately, many of those children are not being correctly diagnosed. As a result, they end up in a program of remediation that is wrong for them, because it addresses the wrong problem. That's why they grow up to become adults who still have the problem to the same extent as when they were children.

It can affect those children. It can even damage their self-image. For example, a lot of those children get the same type of comment each year on their report cards, such as "could do better if tried harder," or "has a lot of potential."

What happens to children who are misdiagnosed? They believe the problem is their own fault. They're the ones to blame. They're the ones not trying hard enough. But they don't know what to do about it. They haven't found any way to bypass the problem, make it go away, or otherwise make things better. Since you cannot depend on the school system or standardized tests to pick up SSS, screening for it takes on more importance. Of course, a child with a reading or learning problem might not have SSS, but it's simple enough to find out.

THE GOAL OF SCREENING

Screening involves obtaining information to determine if SSS is affecting reading and learning. The screeners will be able to know whether the person is scotopic. If there is SSS, the screeners initially will recommend the correct color overlays to reduce the perceptually based problems.

By the end of the screening, the screeners will have a good idea whether the individual is a good candidate for additional treatment, which aspects of the person's reading have the potential to be improved, and which aspects probably are not improvable.

RIGHT TYPES OF QUESTIONS

What questions are asked during the screening process? The screener wants to know exactly what happens when the person is reading. Even children can explain that. A good question or directive might be, "When you start to get frustrated and you want to stop reading, tell me what reading is like."

For example, a child says, "I start to blink a lot." A good questioner doesn't leave it at that. The child should be asked what happened to make her blink. The child might say, "I blink because words run together and become unreadable. When I blink, it spaces the words out. Now I have spaces between the letters and words. I'm able to read just so long, and then everything seems to shift and merge together again. Then I blink and everything goes back to normal again. There comes a point when the blinking stops working, and I have to stop reading." That is very important information. You need the right questions to get that kind of an answer.

Don't teachers normally ask those questions? Unfortunately, they usually don't. Some people feel that teachers do not ask questions when people are stumbling over words because they don't want to break the flow of comprehension. But in general, that is not the reason. More often, it's because teachers truly believe they already know what the answers would be. Because teachers still think that reading involves the basic components of sight vocabulary, phonics, and decoding skills—but involves nothing else—too many of them don't consider that there are other reasons why a child might stumble over or incorrectly read a word.

WHEN TO SCREEN

The ability to diagnose SSS depends on a lot of things. Each symptom or combination of symptoms of Scotopic Sensitivity Syndrome can have a different effect on reading. Factors in the diagnosis of SSS include the severity of the symptoms, the demands of the educational system, the maturity and verbal skills of the individual, the number and severity of other reading difficulties, and what ways the individual has learned to compensate.

Children should be screened for SSS at different times during their school careers. Children who have SSS cannot always be identified as having it. Early detection is important, but immaturity and a lack of verbal skills can hamper the diagnostic process. Therefore, it is important not to rule out SSS as a problem even though initial screenings might be negative.

For example, children in first or second grade who have difficulty learning basic reading skills might be successfully diagnosed if the distortions they are experiencing are readily identifiable and easy to describe. However, some reading problems might not show up until third grade, when the print size decreases and the amount of print on the page increases. In that instance, perceptual distortions would be affecting accuracy and fluency, not the acquisition of skills. If a child is screened only once, before third grade, then SSS might be missed entirely.

Other SSS-related problems might not occur until middle school or later in a child's school career. Those are the times when the demand for sustained reading and concentration increases. Children who had coped with SSS might not be able to get by any longer just by using their listening and verbal skills. When trying to read, they become fatigued, lose comprehension, and must take breaks. So screening needs to take place at that time, too.

Certain problems might not even be identified until

the individual enters college or the work force. Those individuals have developed compensatory strategies, such as avoiding reading or skipping through their reading. It often is not until academic or job success depends on the ability to read pertinent material that their problems become evident.

VISION BEFORE PERCEPTION

Individuals interested in being screened for SSS should first see an optometrist or ophthalmologist and receive a complete visual examination. If it shows they have any visual problems, corrections should be attempted before SSS screening takes place.

When individuals take a routine eye examination, the vision specialist normally assesses acuity, refractive status, and binocular function. When the exam is more than routine, additional tests will analyze the visual system in greater detail and will also evaluate focusing ability and tracking skills. The doctor will also check for the presence of eye diseases.

For SSS treatment to be successful, existing visual problems need to be treated first. Perception skills are based on a solid visual foundation. It is essential for individuals to eliminate all visual problems prior to getting treatment for perception or other learning difficulties.

HOW SCREENING BEGINS

The first step in working with individuals who potentially have SSS is to give them a detailed, in-depth screening designed to determine the existence and magnitude of any of the symptoms of SSS. What is included in the screening? It involves certain tasks that pose trouble for individuals who have Scotopic Sensitivity Syndrome. The tasks also show the types of distortions that occur for the person during normal reading—and it shows them very quickly. For example, somebody might be able to read normally for fifteen to twenty minutes before experiencing distortions. But the distortions will occur almost immediately when that person does the assessment task.

QUESTIONS—LOTS OF QUESTIONS

A number of very thorough and specific questions are asked. Sensory questions are asked; there are questions about home, school, and work environments; and individuals are asked about important details such as reading habits, lighting conditions, unusual reactions to visual stimuli, and the existence of unusual circumstances.

Taking a family history is part of the screening process. Certain indicators in the family history suggest the person might be a candidate. Questions about other family members' reading histories are asked, because of the possible genetic factor in SSS. For example, is there someone else in the family who is a slow reader or avoids reading or gets strain or fatigue from reading?

The assessment examines both objective performance as well as the person's subjective or clinical reporting. In some cases, SSS can affect someone very subtly. People who use compensatory strategies might not seem to be having difficulties. As a result, the answers to the detailed questions are a critical element in diagnosis.

FAMILY JOINS IN

When any person is tested, other family members are included in the screening process. When children are screened, the parents sit in. That is unusual, because in most educational testing situations the parents are not involved. They do not see it happen. They are told about it or given a report afterwards, but they are not there.

There are a number of reasons it is very helpful for one parent or both to be present for SSS screening. It is very educational for the parents. SSS can run in families, and the parents might have other children who will contend with SSS. As parents become aware of the symptoms of SSS and the types of questions that are asked, they become better able to check others in the family for symptoms of Scotopic Sensitivity Syndrome. For example, the parents might not have paid attention to a second child's complaints that reading is tiring or that he or she takes longer than classmates to finish work. Parents might have thought that those complaints were, well, just complaints! But by sitting through the screening process, they might consider whether that child, too, has SSS.

Finally, screeners let the parents try some of the tasks themselves. In some cases, screeners not only identify a child, but identify one of the parents as having the problem! The parents then, often for the first time, see for themselves what a written page is supposed to look like. They might also experience for the first time what reading is supposed to be. Many of those parents might once have said to themselves, "Well, I guess I'm just lazy" or "I just didn't try enough" or "This is what reading is supposed to be like." They can see now how wrong they were. There is no better way to convince someone that the process works than to let that person experience differences, too.

Parents also learn how the treatment would help. That can be very beneficial to parents who had thought no help was available. Adults have a greater understanding of and belief in what their children tell them when they see and experience it for themselves.

Many children feel comforted, supported, and even encouraged by having a parent try some of the activities. And certainly, if the parent has SSS, it makes the child feel less as if he or she is an identified victim. For example, think of how much it can help an anxious child to hear a parent with SSS report what the printed page looks like. The child might look at the parent and say, "Gee, you're worse than I am!" Parent and child now have something in common to talk about. That makes it easier for the child to accept the situation, because he or she feels less different and therefore less likely to try to hide the problem.

Another advantage: If the child tries to avoid using the overlays or the filters and says, "I don't need it" or "It doesn't work," the parent can now say, "Hey, I know it works. I'm using it myself. I know what the difference is. You and I talked about it. I know what you are experiencing, it's real." When parents experience the problem themselves, they better understand what the child is going through. They can be supportive and encourage the child to use the overlays.

UNIQUE SCREENING

The screening procedures used for SSS do not duplicate anything that is being used to test academic problems. SSS is a different area than students were tested for by schoolteachers, school psychologists, or private testing specialists. SSS assessment procedures don't duplicate testing that is being done by professionals who work with children or adults with learning problems. SSS is not part of psychoeducational assessments, nor are SSS problems looked at in standard achievement batteries or any type of psychological batteries that are used with children who have learning or reading problems. But areas that are not typically investigated, such as SSS, can influence learning.

The screening has three parts to it. Part One attempts to determine the way in which SSS has affected reading.

Part One—The Questions

An inefficient reader will typically give certain responses to questions. Those responses also indicate how severe the problem is. They will suggest whether SSS is being experienced—and if it is, whether to a slight, moderate, or severe degree. The person is rated on a continuum.

The questions in the self-test at the beginning of this book are representative of the types of questions asked during the screening process. The questions aim to identify the types of problems that can occur when an individual with SSS is doing required reading rather than pleasure reading. Often, people with reading difficulties have less trouble when reading for pleasure because that's when comprehension and remembering facts and details become less essential.

Fatigue and discomfort typically should not be part of the reading process. Good readers rarely report that strain or fatigue accompanies their reading, regardless of how long they read. Instead, they report that reading is relaxing and enjoyable.

Part Two—The Tasks

The tasks elicit the symptoms of Scotopic Sensitivity Syndrome for the purpose of assessing the individual's perceptual abilities under structured conditions. The activities speed up the onset, intensity, and impact of SSS.

There is an exceptionally wide variety of symptoms that are part of SSS. Each task focuses on a different set of symptoms. Rarely does anyone have the same degree of difficulty with every activity in this section. But it's important to find out which tasks in the section do cause trouble.

Whether an individual can accurately complete a task is not as important as the types of difficulties, if any, experienced when performing the task. (Figure 8.1 illustrates one of the tasks.)

The type of perceptual skills being tested appear to be fully developed by the time the person has finished kindergarten. There appears to be little change or development in those perceptual functions as the child grows older. The perceptual problems do not lessen with maturation. Even children as young as seven years old should be able to complete most of the activities without difficulty.

Part Three—The Overlays

If the questions of Part One and the tasks of Part Two indicate the presence of SSS, then Part Three begins. It consists of trying a series of colored overlays to see which one is most effective at improving reading ability by reducing the visual perceptual symptoms of SSS.

A wide range of color overlays will be used to change the appearance of the printed page. The overlays will have the desired effect only on the person who is seeing distortions. So now, often for the first time, an individual will be able to identify the differences between what he or she experiences and what a good reader experiences. For example, someone can't talk about words rotating, reversing, or inverting if they have never been exposed to words that don't move. Someone can't describe letters that all run together unless the person has experienced what it is like for the letters to have spaces between them and to have larger spaces between words. With the correct colored overlay, the person will see the differences.

The overlays allow the individual with SSS to see and report differences. The overlays also indicate, with accuracy, which aspects of reading improve with the use of overlays and which subskills do not improve and therefore will continue to be problematic. Those other reading prob-

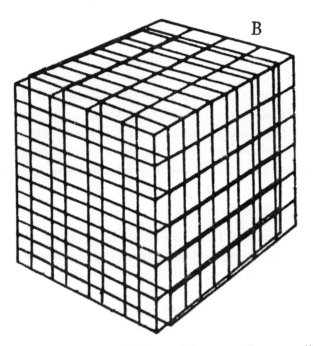

Figure 8.1. In one task, SSS candidates are shown an illustration of a cube and are asked to count the white spaces along the top and down the side of the column marked B. They are then asked to relate whatever difficulties they encountered.

lems will need to be addressed separately, with remediation or other methods.

Remember: Each individual going through the screening process is going to have a different result, depending on what other layers or problems, if any, are contributing to the reading or learning difficulties. The screening will not correct everything for each person who walks in.

By the end of the screening, those with SSS will know which colored overlay to use. In that way, they'll actually have something in hand that they can take away from the testing situation. They'll each take home the colored overlay (or combination of colored overlays) that has proven most helpful. They can use it for a while, independently, to see if it continues to improve their reading. They can work with it to assure themselves that the same type of changes they experienced in the session occur time after time in different environments. They'll watch to see if the changes continue when they read at night, when they read for fifteen or twenty minutes, or when they read in the classroom on a day-to-day basis.

Why is that so important? People who have had an SSS-related problem, especially if it's been for a long time, are probably very skeptical and are frightened to let themselves actually believe that something is going to help them, since nothing has helped them before. Many times in the past, they might have built up their hopes, only to have them crash back down when an attempted remedy didn't prove worthwhile. With the colored overlays, they'll have something in hand with which they can prove to themselves that a process is going to help them.

Once people work with the overlays, they can see changes for themselves. Typically, what they find is that it makes reading a lot easier. They see that if they don't use the overlay, they have a harder time reading (or they just don't want to read), because it's too much work, they make too many errors, and reading is too slow.

After I finally had a name for my problem, things really began to fall into place. It took some of the sting and mystery out of all those years in school where I sat feeling inadequate and unhappy that I couldn't be like the other students.

WHICH COLOR?

Selection of the correct colored overlay or combination of overlays needs to be done by trained professionals who are familiar with SSS symptoms and reading difficulties.

Colored plastic report covers and theatrical gels can change the color of the page, but the most effective overlays are those that do not produce a glare. Overlays that reflect glare might defeat the whole purpose of the process. Any benefits that might otherwise be derived from overlays can be negated if there is glare.

The need for professionals who understand both SSS and reading difficulties cannot be overemphasized. Anybody could try different colors on you, and anybody could try to sell you a bill of goods, but there's much more to it than that. Even a slight change in color can make a big difference. Getting overlays from someone who doesn't understand the method can fall short of the otherwise likely positive outcome, making one believe that the use of color is just another reading-correction process that doesn't work.

Don't try to diagnose yourself or play around with the different colored overlays available. That does not always lead to correct choices. There is no one or two colors that can help everyone. Finding the one right color or combination of colors requires an individual skilled in understanding the complex nature of reading difficulties as well as the symptoms of SSS.

IS SSS PRESENT, AND TO WHAT DEGREE?

The results of the screening quickly provide a good idea whether an individual has SSS and, just as importantly, to what degree.

Some individuals might not show any significant signs of SSS during screening. If a child shows no signs, you can't say definitively that the child is not scotopic. For instance, tests might not detect SSS if a child is unable to report or talk about problems. But as children mature, their reading demands, verbal skills, and awareness all increase; and some of them who previously had, but did not test positively for, SSS might now show signs of it.

Another group is those individuals who seem to have SSS problems but whose other reading problems are so pronounced that it's not clear if treatment for SSS is going to make a significant difference. They'll each be able to take home an overlay and read with it over a period of time. They'll also see if they have more of a desire to sit down and try to read. On the other hand, they might find out that the overlay makes very little difference to them.

A third group is those that clearly have SSS. Within the testing situation, they display all types of problems. They either are very inefficient readers or show a lot of reading fatigue. They have difficulty with performance on the tasks. They see an immediate and dramatic improvement with the overlay. Their reading aloud becomes more confident, more fluent, and has less hesitation and fewer errors. They are able to report clearly what happens on the page when they read without an overlay and the difference the overlay makes.

The final group consists of those who appear to have SSS but do not show improvement with colored overlays. They may choose to go on with the testing, since improvement might occur if the right combination is found among the wide variety of colored filters.

COSTS OF SCREENING

Monetarily, the initial screening process is not expensive. The complete diagnostic examination, including the determination of colored filters but excluding screening, costs $300–$400. The screening by itself is available at a fraction of that cost and lets each person know before investing in the complete process whether it would be beneficial.

With many so-called reading improvement programs,

you don't know whether they're going to work until you've done something over a long period of time and until your money output has become substantial. One of the unique benefits of the SSS program is that any changes that occur with the overlay will be noticed immediately. You'll see them at the screening. When changes occur gradually, you must decide whether to get involved in the process without being sure of the outcome. But you know the outcome immediately with the SSS process. That makes it very different from other interventions.

The screening process gives a clear understanding of which basic reading skills are being held back by SSS and which skills might not improve.

Sometimes, climbing the mountain on the way to success means finding an easier path, but it still can be hard and treacherous. Sometimes, the overlay works like giving ropes and equipment to the mountain climber. It makes the journey less tedious and less difficult, but it will still take effort, guidance, and practice to get to the top of the mountain.

MOVING TO PINPOINTING AND FILTERS

Who moves to the next stage of the process? The screening stage identifies those people who have noticeable improvements when reading with colored overlays. The differences can involve any or all of the reading problems that might be affected by SSS, such as difficulties with sustained reading; a slow reading rate; a poor reading accuracy; and a lack of comfort, ease, and efficiency of reading. Positive results from the screening stage of this process indicate that the individual should go for further diagnostic tests and treatment.

The stage after screening involves determining which color to craft a lens so that it best helps the individual's perception. The colored lenses are not called glasses, but filters, distinguishing them from eyeglasses, which are worn to correct vision problems.

Does improvement in reading with overlays mean that you will benefit from colored filters? Most of the time, but not always. A very small group of individuals cannot tolerate looking through color. They might go through the testing process for filters and still end up using a colored overlay.

Individuals also have the choice not to proceed any further. They can stop after the screening stage and just continue to use the overlay. However, most people find the overlays become cumbersome and restrictive. Colored lenses worn as glasses, on the other hand, have greater versatility. They can improve depth perception and sports performance and can make it easier to read under fluorescent lighting, read music, take tests, and face many other problem situations for those with SSS.

Now that I've outlined the screening process for SSS, you might be interested in looking at a representative sample of what printed material would look like with color.

This is not an actual test. Remember, when SSS interferes with reading ability, a number of variables are involved, such as lighting, glare, and color. Other than in a formal screening session, it would be impossible to control all variables to determine the effects of color.

1 An Introduction: General Strategy

The general strategy behind *Love Tactics* is quite simple. It is based on the premise that romantic love has three essential parts: 1. *Friendship* 2. *Respect* and 3. *Passion*. Because love will fail if it lacks one or more of these necessary ingredients, the only way you can be successful in winning the one you want is by learning how to cultivate *all three feelings* in their heart for you.

THE HOUSE OF LOVE

We can compare a love relationship to a housing unit. As long as it is complete and functions the way it should, it makes a pleasant abode. There is no incentive to move out, since all one's needs for shelter and comfort are being adequately met.

But what if the resident came home, night after night, only to discover that there was no roof? Or floor? Or walls? It wouldn't be long before they would be looking for a new home!

Sometimes, out of desperation, a person may jump prematurely into a situation that meets some of their more immediate needs. But if this situation doesn't satisfy their other emotional requirements as well, they will eventually realize their mistake (and move out)!

AN EMPTY HOUSE

Why does love sometimes fail? In most cases it can be traced to the absence of one or more of these three essential elements. Together, these elements contain all the ingredients necessary for the development of romantic fulfillment. Just as a house would be incomplete without a roof, walls, or foundation, so would a relationship be unfulfilling without friendship, respect, and passion. If just one of these components fails to germinate and develop, then the person lacking these feelings for the other cannot help but feel a little dissatisfied (yes, even cheated!). The relationship would be about as rewarding as sitting down on a three-legged stool and finding out (too late) that it only has two legs!

The basic strategy, then, to win *and* keep the one you want is to cultivate *friendship, respect,* and *passion* in your relationship with that person. *Only* when all three of these essential elements are present can you hope to enjoy love at its very best!

FRIENDSHIP

Before you can truly win someone's heart, you must first become friends with that person. Although this may appear easy, it really is not. True friendship meets a person's deep, emotional needs. A wise person once defined *a friend* as "someone you can think out loud in front of." In light of this definition, then, we might all find ourselves reevaluating who we really consider to be our true friends!

To become a true friend, you must learn to meet that person's basic human emotional needs. These include:

1. *Attention.* You'll need to show the other person that you are consciously aware of his or her existence.

2. *Understanding.* Just communicating your awareness that the person exists isn't enough. You also need to show that you're aware of how *they feel* about—and perceive—the world around them.

3. *Acceptance.* This means showing the person that you still value being with them, even though at times their behavior or attitudes may be less than praiseworthy.

4. *Appreciation.* You can satisfy this need by recognizing those redeeming qualities that the other person possesses.

5. *Affection.* This is easily shown by reassuring the person that, regardless of comparisons with others, he or she is still very special to you and, therefore, very important. Sometimes this can be communicated by no more than a *simple touch.*

As you begin to meet a person's five basic emotional friendship needs, you'll be helping that person along the road to greater happiness. In return, he or she will develop a subconscious emotional dependence on you. This dependence is an essential part of any romantic relationship. In order to encourage them to voluntarily place this trust in you, however, you must first prove worthy of their trust.

Behavior Principle #1:
People Subconsciously Grow Dependent Upon Those Who Satisfy Their Emotional Needs

The first objective of *Love Tactics* is to show you how to satisfy the emotional friendship needs of the one you want—and to do it better and more completely than anyone they have ever met before! The various techniques described in this book will help you to easily accomplish this.

RESPECT

While it is true that pure *friendship* is the engine of romantic love, *respect* is the gas that makes it go! People are motivated to be with, and to associate themselves with, those persons whom they truly respect.

How do we come to respect someone? Respect is an acquired attitude. For the most part, it is usually based on our perception of a person's independence and self-reliance. The more capable a person seems to be of getting along in life without having to rely on us, the more likely we are to actually feel drawn towards that person. The opposite also holds true. The more easily a person becomes dependent upon us, the more "turned off" we become. When people act possessive towards us and show an inclination to "cling," our degree of respect for them declines. It is quite normal to feel a need to escape from such persons.

Behavior Principle #2:
People Are Most Attracted To Those Who Exhibit Some Degree Of Aloofness and Self-Reliant Independence

So if we want to win someone's heart fully and completely, we must be perceived (by that person) as being capable of surviving quite well without him or her. At the same time, however, we cannot neglect their very real psychological need for friendship. This presents us with the task of performing a delicate balancing act. Again, *Love Tactics* will show you how to accomplish both objectives!

PASSION

The crowning experience of romantic love is the ultimate sensation we know as *passion*. We can only enjoy something in life to the degree that we truly long for it. Therefore, levels of romantic desire must be raised to a fever pitch if the romantic experience is really going to satisfy our need for a fulfilling relationship and become the ecstasy we always dreamed of. This brings us to one of the most widely-known principles of human behavior.

Behavior Principle #3:
People Want What They Can't Have!

What happens when people become overly confident that a desirable object is "theirs for the taking?" They'll almost always take such a treasure for granted. (Frequently, they'll even abuse it!) Therefore, if you want to successfully build a romantic relationship with someone, it is imperative that you not ignore this principle. Otherwise, you will wind up forfeiting the rewards that you would ultimately have reaped!

By using the tactics discussed in the remainder of this book, you can build a romantic fire in someone else's heart that will blaze exclusively for *you*. Once begun, this fire will burn so brightly that the remaining embers will continue to glow for a lifetime! So there is no time like the present to concentrate on fueling that fire with the appropriate elements.

The secret to building passion in another person can be expressed in the form of a mathematical equation:

$$HOPE + DOUBT = PASSION$$

COMMITMENT

Falling in love is ultimately a rational, conscious act. It's a willful decision to let down our last remaining emotional barriers and become wholly vulnerable to another human being. But even though this final decision is a conscious and rational act, it is actually based upon emotional feeling, despite the natural tendency to deny this. As J. Pierpont Morgan reportedly once quipped, "Every man has two reasons for doing, or not doing, a thing: One that sounds good, and a real one."

Behavior Principle #4:
People Make Conscious Decisions Based On Subconscious Feelings, Then Justify Their Decisions With Reasons That Sound Good

It doesn't matter how logical it seems that a particular person should be in love with you. If the proper emotional attitudes have not been cultivated inside that person, then a meaningful commitment to you in a relationship simply will not occur. It is true that a person may commit himself to you based on sheer will power alone, but that person would always feel a void and emptiness inside. This would undermine the strength of anyone's commitment to you in the long run, no matter how sincere it might be at first.

On the other hand, if the proper feelings of friendship, respect, and passion have been appropriately cultivated in the relationship, it would be practically impossible for the person to resist making such a commitment to you, regardless of other "logical" reasons why it shouldn't happen.

If it's your desire to truly be loved by the one you want—if you want a complete, fulfilling, and totally reciprocated commitment from the person of your dreams—then get smart! Use the understanding of human behavior you will acquire from this book to your advantage! Cultivate friendship, respect, and passion in your relationship, and you will see how commitment to you will follow as naturally as day follows night!

Simply put, the general strategy of this book is based on the philosophy, *"love begets love."* The key is to communicate that love. It begins with your commitment to love another human being. It results in that person's commitment to love you back.

2 *Acting With Self-Assurance*

Now you're ready to begin! You're willing to give it a try and go after the one you want! You're hopeful that this book will finally unravel the mystery of how to do it! But deep down you're still wondering if you've got what it takes. You have self-doubts. You're afraid.

Let those fears be dispelled! True enough, *you* are where this whole process begins. But *we* have faith in you! We know from our own personal experience that you (whoever you are) have within you capacities for greatness yet untapped! We haven't the slightest doubt that you, in fact, are *already* great—however hidden from view this side of you may have been until now.

This chapter contains a number of tactics that will help you to feel more confident about yourself. As this confidence grows, you will become more emotionally prepared to successfully win the one you want. Additionally, you will radiate more charm to help enchant and draw the one you want *to you*.

Whitney Houston sings that "learning to love yourself is the greatest love of all . . . " It is understandable that, unless a person feels good about himself, then he will not be able to show much love to another person. Therefore, it's important for you to learn to *like yourself* as much as possible. Our whole focus here can be summed up in the words *positive self-image*.

VIBES

Have you ever noticed that people tend to pick up vibes from others they are with? Think about the people you enjoy being with the most. You undoubtedly pick up positive vibes from these people, and that's why you enjoy being with them. So it makes sense for you to try to radiate these same types of positive vibes to others. But how is this done? Again, *by feeling better about yourself.* A positive self-image gives off positive vibes. This will be apparent in your face, your speech, and your behavior in general.

The vibes you give off will become an "aura" that brightens the atmosphere around you, engulfing and captivating those individuals with whom you come in contact. Others will enjoy being with you because of your positive attitude. This is the true source of that personal magnetism we know of as *charisma.*

LOVE TACTIC #1 Be Nice To Number One (Yourself)!

Before you can begin to glow with increased self-confidence, you must practice treating yourself with kindness, tolerance, and mercy! Research has indicated that many people are harder on themselves than they need be. They are too negative and self-critical in their private thoughts. Constantly bad-mouthing yourself will only serve to keep your self-image low. And, consequently, such self-deprecation can also diminish a person's ability to win the one they want.

So cut it out! As a first step toward winning the one you want, commit yourself here and now to break any such patterns of self-abuse. Make up your mind to no longer put yourself down. From now on, it is essential that you *go easier on yourself and be nice to Number One (yes, that's you!)* True, you may not be perfect, but it is vital to the overall plan that you at least treat yourself with respect.

How do you begin, if such self put-downs are already a habit with you? First, become consciously aware of exactly how much you do this. Take note of when you say something negative to yourself. Mentally keep track of your personal thoughts and self-dialogues. What did you say? What were your reasons for being upset with yourself?

Even if you get angry at something you've done, realize that you can learn from your mistakes. You *can* change. Criticize your *behavior* instead of blaming *yourself.* Emphasize the action rather than the person. How much better it is to say, "I did a dumb thing" than "I'm dumb!" Turn those negatives around! You can always find something positive in yourself.

Sure, this requires letting yourself off the hook sometimes when you blow it. But who doesn't deserve a good dose of mercy from time to time? And we promise that the improvement you will see in yourself because of this will surpass any results you hope to achieve by self-chastisement! In this way, you'll gradually improve the way you feel about yourself. As you feel more confident, it will begin to show and the people around you will respond to the aura that you radiate.

This is not to say that you should engage in the practice of excusing your faults, or bragging to others. Just realize that everyone has faults. Making mistakes does not make you a "bad" person. In fact, being human can actually work in your favor. As one young single person explained, "I don't want someone who is *too* perfect!"

Second, realize that nobody is perfect. Everyone (absolutely *everyone*) makes mistakes and, heck, you are certainly entitled to your share of them! Mistakes do not make a person inferior—only human!

Third, don't become discouraged if you're having a hard time shaking your feelings of inferiority, even after what we've just told you in the paragraph above! Be aware that if you are plagued with a bit of an inferiority complex, you are not alone. In fact, *most* people in the world secretly feel inferior to others, though they obviously don't go around broadcasting this. So your feelings of inadequacy are *not* the end of the world. You can *still* win the one you want, in spite of this. Millions of others have! But the more accepting you are of yourself, *without putting yourself down*, the greater an advantage you will have.

Fourth, realize that no matter what frailties you may have exhibited in the past, if you are capable of *recognizing* them as faults then you possess the capacity to improve yourself. This is a very important point.

Last, control your inner thinking. Indulging in negative thoughts can be one of the most destructive things you do.

(Text on the colored pages comes from *Love Tactics: How to Win the One You Want*, by Thomas W. McKnight and Robert H. Phillips, Avery Publishing Group, 1988. Reprinted with permission.)

9.

Pinpointing and Treating SSS

For those individuals who have been diagnosed as having SSS, the next part of the process is very exciting. A much more precise, comprehensive, diagnostic process takes place. Its purpose is to identify exactly which distortions are occurring and then, based on that, to determine which color will work best in the filters.

More than 25,000 people are wearing colored filters as a specific treatment for SSS around the world. Thousands more are using just colored overlays to reduce the impact of SSS.

WHY COLOR SELECTION IS SO IMPORTANT

People with SSS can experience a variety of distortions when they read. By using the technique of spectral modification with colored lenses, all—not just some—of the distortions will be reduced or eliminated. That makes perceptual activities easier, resulting in improved reading and comprehension. Eliminating the print and/or back-ground distortions, increasing the span of recognition, and keeping letters and words readable can promote greater comfort and duration of reading. The amount of improve-ment resulting from the use of spectral modification will be influenced by the degree of involvement of SSS and the presence or absence of other factors that can cause reading problems.

For those who suffer from SSS, the problem can be experienced on a continuum, from slight, to moderate, to severe. Even good readers with SSS can benefit from spectral modification. Their quality of life, achievement of goals, and ease of accomplishment can be increased with the use of colored filters or overlays.

For individuals with SSS who are poor readers, learn-ing disabled, or have visual dyslexia, the simple process of adding color can make a world of difference. Since the perceptual distortions can be many and varied and severe, the improvement can be substantial.

Remember that the goal is to filter selectively that part of the color spectrum, and only that small amount of light, that seems to be causing the brain to distort the informa-tion it receives. Because that light varies from person to person, there are literally hundreds and hundreds of dif-ferent colors or combinations of colors but only one that will be helpful. To come up with an approximate color, but not the right one, would be a waste of time, energy, and money. Because there are so many color combinations, the diagnostic questions that help pinpoint the exact nature of the perceptual problems are critical. The process for de-termining the right color is precise, intense, and often lengthy. In some cases, it can take two hours or more. But—it's worth it! Selecting the correct filter color is the most important component of the entire process.

BEWARE: OVERLAY COLOR ≠ FILTER COLOR

Interestingly, the color that works best in the filters differs from the one that worked best in the person's overlays. The reason for that is not totally clear, but there are some thoughts on the matter.

The colored overlay that is placed directly on the page affects only the reflected light from the page and does not modify the environmental lighting. But when a person wears colored filters, all light entering the eye is modified. When the overlay is down on the page, the color of the background becomes the color of the overlay; but when filters are worn, the page stays white.

Tinting filters to the color of the overlay might not be helpful. More likely than not, distortions would persist and might even be made worse.

USE AN EXPERT

It's essential to recognize that an individual should not try to determine by himself or herself what the correct color should be. Most people with SSS are not aware of what the printed page is supposed to look like when they're reading. They are not aware, therefore, of what type of problems they are having. If they try to determine a tint themselves, they might pick a color for the wrong reasons. They might, for example, pick a color just because it is their favorite or because it is colorful! They would not necessarily pick the color that is most beneficial to them in reducing distortions.

Although most individuals experience a large number of problems, they usually are aware of only the predominant one. Finding the color that seems to help only one of their problems will not be optimal.

To determine color, therefore, it is necessary to form an individual profile. Experts need to identify all of the problems that occur, and they need to get rid of all, not just a few, of them. That's the only way the process can work and be truly beneficial.

Many vision specialists have the capability to tint lenses. They do cosmetic tinting. They will give you a color that looks appealing or let you pick your own color. They might even say that pink is the best color to use if you have problems with fluorescent lighting. If you have learned nothing else, you are now aware that there are no universal colors for everyone who has SSS. Each individual needs a color that is adapted specifically for him or her.

The use of colored filters as a treatment for reading and other academic problems is not the same as simply using cosmetically colored glasses for comfort or attractiveness. As a treatment technique it is a science that requires persons competent in analyzing reading difficulties, understanding academic problems, and knowing the relationship of SSS to reading and learning. You might end up in a color that brings little benefit if you deal with someone who cannot diagnose you to determine what problems are interfering with reading and who does not have a background in reading disabilities to determine the type and extent of benefits that should occur.

Worse, yet, you might mistakenly believe that you do not have SSS, because the person doing the tinting does not have the training or background to know if you need color or which color is best.

Many individuals do not know why they cannot read, why they find reading boring, or why they avoid reading. They just know it is hard and frustrating. Most of the time, they believe they are just not trying hard enough. Couple that with a lack of knowledge about the true nature of their reading problem (obscure perceptual distortions) and it becomes clear why no one but a trained diagnostician will be able to detect Scotopic Sensitivity Syndrome.

For cosmetic tinting, an individual selects the color that is most appealing, but for SSS the color is carefully and diagnostically prescribed; the filters are then tinted to meet the specifications on the prescription. In both cases, the mechanics of tinting are basically the same.

If they are to remedy reading problems, filters must be matched exactly to the prescribed color. That takes anywhere from forty-five minutes to a day and a half. The process is carefully monitored by using a photospectrometer, which graphs the prescribed color and matches it to the created filter. Even differences of color too slight to be seen will reduce or eliminate all the benefits of the program. An individual who has the equipment to do cosmetic tinting is not necessarily trained or equipped to provide the required accuracy to the tint. Repeatedly, individuals have complained that they have hired vision specialists who claimed they could tint lenses to treat SSS and that the resulting lenses might have looked good but just didn't work.

WHAT HAPPENS AFTER TREATMENT?

For many individuals with SSS, as soon as they start wearing their appropriately colored filters, sustained reading time changes dramatically.

BEFORE
I love information, but I hate to read. It takes me so long to read I hardly ever get it done in time. I have to stay up real late to finish my homework, but if I want to get to college I have to read.

AFTER
I love these! It's like all of it is there—nice clear

paper—not muddy gray—nice printed words, and they're all there. It's clear, and nothing moves outward. It's absolutely perfect. It's like someone opened the blinds for me and let in the light for the first time.

BEFORE

My eyes burn and itch. The print pops out and moves around and around like a carousel. Sometimes the print looks like a picket fence, and there are flickers and flashes of light.

AFTER

I love it! Now it feels like words just float into my head. There's nothing moving or swirling, and everything is flat and still. It stops my eyes from hurting and makes it so much easier to read. No one should have to go through what I went through.

BEFORE

Sometimes some of the words just go away, and then everything else moves all over. There's little lights all over the pages, and words jump up and down. It's like being snow-blind.

AFTER

I used to fight to get words. Now they just pour into my head. I never realized how bad the page looked before I had something to compare it to.

BEFORE

The words and lines turn sideways and look like waves, then they move together in a big black line. Hey! This whole line just went off the page.

AFTER

I can read! I read every one of these words, and they stayed where they're supposed to! It's like someone lifted the lid and I could see what was inside.

BEFORE

Everything hurts my eyes, and my head hurts as soon as I look at the page. Sometimes it makes me sick to my stomach. I hardly ever read, because it hurts. All those lines slide down the front. This page looks like there's a thousand ants with lights on them running across the page.

AFTER

I grew up feeling something was wrong. Now I know that is not true. Now, nothing is moving, the words don't scrunch together, and my headache is gone. It takes away all the lights. I like it. I can read with these on. It's a nice feeling to know that my reading problems are something I don't have to live with.

These comments were made after treatment with colored filters:

I couldn't read without leaving out words. I used to skip words and sentences and couldn't read for more than five to ten minutes. It was very frustrating for me. Once I wore the filters the change was so rapid it was unbelievable. I could now read as long as I wanted. One day I read for two hours. I've never been able to do that before. I actually felt sad about finishing the book.

The only thing that I read before I got my filters was the TV guide in the local newpaper. When I got them, I rushed to my husband's office, opened up a book, and started to read like I have never read before. He actually picked me up and swung me around. He was so excited for me. I then rushed

*out and bought myself a novel and actually compre-
hended what I had read and absolutely enjoyed
every moment.*

*Before I had my colored glasses, my concentration
was really bad. I would read something, and it
would not stay in my mind. Also, in class, what the
teacher said would go in one ear and out the other.
When I did my math, the numbers would cross over
columns, and I would always get the math wrong.
When I first got my lenses, I was shy to wear them
because they are orange. But now the other kids
don't even notice them. Because I have improved
so much, other kids that have reading problems
like mine want to get some, too.*

*Richard is a new child. When he forgets to wear his
glasses and tries to read, it's obvious from the first
hesitant word that he's not wearing his 'special
glasses.' They make such an enormous difference.
My husband and I are delighted for Richard, but
we are just as delighted for ourselves. We don't
have to endure the agony of seeing our son struggle
with reading and low self-esteem.*

*It's made all the difference in the world! Reading
used to be so frustrating that I would throw books,
scream, and yell. In work the difference has been
[my going] from not successful to very successful. I
now am able to get the information I need to do my
job. It's like night and day.*

*I never knew what the problem was, but I always
lost my place. I had to read things several times to
understand what I was reading. Now I can read
across a line or sentence and know what it means. I
can find something because I can see it distinctly in
what used to be a sea of letters. It's hard to believe*

that this makes such a difference. I'm not just dumb or unable to learn to read—I can read.

To get the glasses with the colored lenses was the best thing in the world. It was like I was raised in solitary confinement and the glasses opened the door. I am 37 years old and am just now seeing the world the way it really is.

It was at the university that the problems began. I could not cope with the reading load. I needed to read closely, but it was precisely what I couldn't do. In order to understand material, I had to read and reread many times. But I could only read for a few minutes at a time. Essay writing was impaired because I could not do the necessary reading and research. My marks on exams were poor. The difference has been dramatic. For the first time in my life, I do not always feel tired and ill. I can read textbooks and understand without having to reread. I can read for longer periods of time and concentrate more easily. The lenses have changed my life in a way that I didn't think was possible.

FILTERS ALONE ARE NOT ALWAYS SUFFICIENT

Just to prescribe colored filters would be doing some individuals a great disservice. In some cases, perceptual problems will be reduced but not totally eliminated by the use of colored filters. For the use of color to provide full benefits, it sometimes is necessary to combine colored filters with other ways of modifying light. That is similar to not treating cancer by surgery alone if you knew that the patient was more likely to get well if you were to combine the surgery with chemotherapy and/or radiation therapy. You do not want to be given colored filters alone if you need more.

White paper is so difficult to look at in some cases that it must be totally eliminated, even for individuals wearing colored filters. Instead, colored paper must be used for writing letters and assignments and taking notes and tests. The choice of color must be carefully determined. Some colors will make reading harder, while others in combination with the filters will make reading easier.

The lighting, the chair, the angle at which books are held, and the size of the print are all important factors that can be modified to help the person with SSS even more.

Even with colored filters, some individuals need to continue using overlays for reading under certain lighting conditions. Colored filters alone can be beneficial for many situations, but the addition of the overlay when reading might mean even greater improvement. That requires additional selection procedures, though, because the choice of overlay color changes when used in combination with colored filters.

OTHER LAYERS IN LEARNING PROBLEMS

Any diagnosis for, or treatment of, SSS would not be complete without investigating some of the other layers that might contribute to reading or learning problems. It would be remiss to look at SSS in isolation. Diagnostic procedures check for any problem area that might affect learning, not just for SSS. When problems are found in other areas, the possible involvement of SSS should be assessed. When SSS is not contributing to, or causing, those problems, then strong recommendations are made that need to be implemented both at home and in school or at work. Those recommendations usually take the form of educational strategies that might need to be used for the rest of that person's life.

Educators generally concentrate on skill building, and

they often view strategies as crutches. As such, many educators feel that strategies should be eliminated from the educational environment. They might fear that using such strategies would prohibit the development of skills.

In some people, certain skills will never develop adequately to allow for academic success. In my research studies, the adults with learning disabilities who were able to enter college were those who fought the system and developed their own strategies. It was the development and use of those strategies that made the difference between academic success and failure.

Remember that Scotopic Sensitivity Syndrome is rarely found as a problem in isolation. There can be other learning problems involved.

10.

Bringing It All Together

O K, the screening and treatment have both been completed, and the individual has gotten tinted filters, alone or with other aids. Now what happens?

The results and consequences are going to be different for each individual. Many factors must be considered, because learning is not a simple concept. There are many layers to learning. Reading problems might not be related to other academic deficits and can have many causes that coexist. Each individual has different strengths and weaknesses. All those factors contribute to the success or amount of success that individuals experience with colored filters.

WHAT IF SSS IS THE ONLY PROBLEM?

The ideal scenario would be for an individual to have SSS as the only problem, with all the other areas in relatively good shape.

Some people who have SSS have reading difficulties

only because perceptual distortions are interfering with their ability to read. They have already developed many good skills, even if they have not been able to use or incorporate all of them because of SSS. They have adequate sight vocabulary skills and decoding skills; they are able to read, to use context clues, and to comprehend information; they can distinguish between nonmeaningful and meaningful, essential and nonessential details. Once you take away the perceptual problems, all the skills fall into place, and those people are able to utilize them.

What Happens to Them After Treatment?

They are the lucky group! As a result of treatment, they will notice dramatic changes. They might have to get used to a new way of reading. For example, they might have to get used to reading more rapidly. They might not be used to seeing more than three letters when they read, being able to scan a page and get meaning while they do it, or reading without constantly stopping. It might take a while for them to accept that words have meaning and that reading doesn't necessitate rereading material three or four times. They'll be changing some reading patterns that they had developed to compensate for their SSS. They're not automatically going to drop them. They're going to have to learn to trust the process, to experience the difference, to trust the difference. There is a period of adjustment, even to something good!

WHAT IF SSS IS NOT THE ONLY PROBLEM?

The next group (which is more common) is the group of individuals who have problems in addition to SSS. The greater the number of problems, the less dramatic the differences will be. SSS becomes only one piece of the puzzle. For those individuals with other reading or learning problems, SSS treatment is going to focus on only the perceptual component. For example, if a word is unknown, just because it becomes legible doesn't mean it will be instantly recognized. Individuals in this group might need to continue remediation or seek out other educational interventions to deal with the other types of learning and reading problems that they have.

Reading might remain a problem despite the readability of the page. Reading might still be a frustrating and complicated task. Vocabulary skills might be limited and require remediation. The reader might still need to develop analytical reading skills to understand subtleties and interpret the material. Reading is very complex.

This group includes some children who are still in elementary school. Because of perceptual interference, they have not picked up the basic reading skills that they need to learn. Those children, then, need to go back through the basic skills that haven't had a chance to develop. Parents must not assume that the skills that have been taught in the past have actually been learned.

Let's take an example. Some children with SSS, when they're reading, find that the white background takes over letters and parts of letters. But it's not going to take over letters only. The background might also make it virtually impossible to see other things on the page, like periods, commas, and other punctuation marks. One of the activities taken for granted in reading has been understanding how to use punctuation marks. When people who are reading reach a comma, they're supposed to let their voice pause. A problem occurs if they've never seen any punctuation marks! So when, for the first time, they're able to see them, they have to learn anew what they mean. And of course, they need to learn how to use them when they write, too.

Some students learned to read even though they did not see all the letters in the word. They might have seen letters at the beginning and at the end, but the letters in the middle were dancing and switching around too much to be seen. Using the colored filters, the students might say, "Oh, that's what that word looks like!" So now they'll be able to build up their vocabulary and match the visual image to the sound of the word. Also, spelling can improve when each word has a consistent visual image.

When Other Problems Overshadow SSS

In some cases, SSS will have even less of an impact. In those instances, correction for SSS might mean that individuals will be able to work on a task longer. It might not mean that they're going to read any better or that reading is going to be any easier or any more automatic. Those individuals have other, more severe reading or learning problems, and remediation will need to continue on a long-term basis.

Children who continue to have extreme reading problems after SSS problems are corrected will need to continue other therapies. When SSS is corrected, all the distortions will be reduced or eliminated. So those children will be able to work longer, concentrate on building skills, and enjoy not having perceptual problems interfering with their trying to learn how to read. Remediation and other educational interventions are essential.

Adults with the same type of problem are in a different situation. They might have so adapted their lifestyle to avoid reading that unless there is a fast and big change in their reading ability they will continue to get by without reading, will do minimal amounts of reading, or will use compensatory strategies such as having other people read to them. For example, a 34-year-old man who despite tutoring and remediation has a reading level of approximately the second grade wanted to put on the colored filters and immediately be able to read. But the distortions he had experienced on the page were minimal and contributed more to discomfort than interference with reading. He would not be a good candidate for filters, because his reading level would not increase greatly and therefore the likelihood that he would read would be minimal.

HAVING SSS BUT NOT FINDING A SOLUTION

About 6 percent of the individuals who have SSS and appear to be good candidates to be helped by the filters cannot be helped. They seem to meet all the criteria, but overlays or filters do not make much of a difference for them. Regardless of what is tried, their problems are going to remain. So, you might ask, why should they bother going for diagnosis?

If they have SSS and they don't go, then they'll never know whether they're in the 6 percent who can't be helped or the 94 percent who can. (And chances are they'll be in the 94 percent.) Even if treatment can't remedy their SSS, at least they'll stop blaming themselves. It can be helpful for them to know why reading has been difficult and not successful. They can stop thinking that they're doing something wrong, that they should be doing something differently, or that they need to try harder. If they're still in school, it allows school personnel to make appropriate recommendations for placement. In some instances, they might redirect the individual to use alternative methods for reading, such as having someone record books on tape or read to them.

Kevin was a child who desperately wanted to go to college. He had been told that he needed to be able to read. He spent most of his school career with special tutors and reading experts, but reading remained a severe problem. At age 16, he became suicidal because of his inability to make progress in reading. He saw only one letter at a time and, for him, that could not be improved. Once the problem was identified, the school realized that remediation would not improve Kevin's reading and allowed him oral tests and taped books. Three years later, he is finishing his first year of college on the honor roll.

HOLDOUTS

Many people continue to believe that any problem that exists can be corrected by remediation or maturation. They do not believe that SSS is a real problem; the child just needs to work harder. But SSS is real. It won't go away. And, without correction, it can have a direct and continuing impact on the reading and learning process.

Surprisingly, not everyone rushes to be helped by treatment for SSS, even if they know they can be helped. Why? There seems to be a lot of fear and even denial. Instead of approaching it positively and wanting to do something about it, the reaction might be very different. People might deny the problem exists or refuse to be tested. Some people feel it's easier or more comfortable to plan their lives around what they already know. Even if what they know is difficult, leads to failure, or requires compensatory stategies, at least they know what is going on and what to expect.

So some people reject the process because they are not sure they want to change. They are not sure what change would mean to their lives. They are not sure if they would be able to handle change or the new expectations that would come from change. They might wonder, if the process really changes their abilities and they no longer keep on failing, would people start expecting them to succeed?

How would they deal with that? What do they do if people now expect them to succeed, and they can't? That's why people sometimes persist in doing what they've done all along instead of seeking out change. In a way, that is a fear of success.

PATTERN OF SUCCESS

Actual change incorporates a little success, then fear, then failure, then trying again, then failing again. Part of any progress incorporates at least a year of success, failure, success, and more failure. Real change takes a number of years.

Parents and teachers have expectations that when something is changed, the child's grades will immediately show improvement. But failure or poor performance is going to continue for a while, although that doesn't mean the process doesn't work. If they monitor the child's progress, they'll find that even though the child is failing at times, the child is also succeeding at times. The successes become more and more a part of the child's academic pattern. The successes become stronger and better.

Each failing experience provides important learning that tends to help increase the likelihood of success in subsequent experiences. So parents and teachers shouldn't jump on the child, pointing out each failure. Instead, they should compliment the child on each success.

FACTORS INHIBITING SUCCESS

Colored filters can be very helpful by minimizing interference from the print or the background, thereby improving visual perception for tasks such as reading and writing. However, that doesn't guarantee that all aspects of an existing learning or reading problem will improve once the distortions are minimized or eliminated.

Many factors can restrict the degree to which a person, despite improvement in visual perceptual skills because of colored filters, will improve in reading, writing, and other academic skills.

Once distortions have been eliminated, good reading practices must be developed to build skills in deficient areas. Only by doing that will a person's interest in reading grow, which helps the individual develop even more advanced skills.

Peer Pressure

The importance of peer pressure in our society is well documented. People tend to cover up areas of inadequacy so that members of their peer group will be less likely to notice those deficiencies. Peer pressure tends to be most prevalent among adolescents. Acceptance by friends might be more important to a youth than using a technique that can improve performance in school. As a result, many individuals with SSS might be reluctant to wear colored filters because it can focus undesirable attention on their problem.

Why are they concerned? Because people who have reading or learning problems are commonly thought of as having intelligence problems, even if that is totally untrue. In fact, research has indicated that individuals with learning disabilities have average, if not above average, intelligence. But people with chronic learning problems often develop a sensitivity about their learning difficulties, along with a lack of confidence.

What can be done? Because of the importance of both peer group acceptance and visual perceptual improvement, a compromise might well be discussed for those children with SSS who because of peer pressure don't want to wear filters. Instead of filters being used all the time, it might be better to select specific situations where they can be used with a minimum of attention. At least, in that way, both important needs are being met.

Behavior and Confidence Problems

Children with SSS probably have a more difficult and frustrating time with schoolwork than those who don't have SSS. A great deal of energy and effort might produce marginally successful results. And, after all their efforts, the comments received from peers and teachers might be far from complimentary. After having to endure negative attention for prolonged periods of time, is it any wonder that many individuals with SSS have low self-esteem and display problem behavior?

Why might such students act up? If a child is having trouble focusing on work and difficulty achieving in the classroom, it would not be surprising for that student to start talking to classmates, copying work from others, daydreaming, distracting other children, and so on. Teachers, of course, would not be thrilled to see that occur. Negative feelings toward children who regularly behave that way would not be surprising.

Even after colored filters have improved the students' ability to read successfully, support and encouragement from both family and school will be necessary to reduce inappropriate behavior patterns and improve the children's self-confidence. Whereas the children might now be able to read written text, they undoubtedly will still need time and support to feel good about themselves and change their behavior. Until that can be achieved, emotional support must continue.

Avoidance Habits

Because of the difficulties experienced from SSS, the child has probably learned to avoid doing schoolwork, homework, reading, and studying. After all, why do something that you just can't seem to do well, no matter how much effort you put into it? Compensatory strategies and excuses become protective devices to keep others off their backs.

Once many of the symptoms of SSS are eliminated and reading becomes more possible, the avoidance habits that have been developed over the years must also be changed. Since all habits are resistant to change, the task will not be easy or quick.

HOW SCHOOLS CAN HELP

It's important that educators and other professionals in the school system realize that there are a lot of ways that individuals with SSS can be helped in school. That is especially important because so many of those individuals have a great deal of potential—largely untapped.

Certain lighting and colors can present problems for students with SSS, but many things can be done in school to ease those problems. For example? Paper color can be changed, color contrast can be modified, the intensity of light can be reduced, and attention can be paid to illumination and glare.

Lighting

Students with SSS are able to read more comfortably, more effectively, and for longer periods of time when under dimmer lighting or under lighting that is either natural or incandescent. Fluorescent is the most difficult lighting for those with SSS to read under, since it hastens the onset, as well as adds to the intensity, of the distortions.

Steps can be taken against the problems people with SSS have from glare and lighting intensity. For example, some people have found bookstands helpful in reducing glare. Books held on such stands can be propped at a comfortable angle, thereby reducing the glare of light off the page.

The use of visors (or even hats or caps with brims) can shield the eyes from glare and improve the ability of those with SSS to read. But it takes a willingness on the part of the school system to allow an exception to the usual rule that no head coverings be worn in school.

Classroom teachers might consider unscrewing some of the fluorescent lights or, even better, turning out the lights nearest a window so that some of the students can read by natural light.

Paper Color

The contrast of black print on white paper has always been judged to be best for most readers. But for those with SSS, it's the worst! It precipitates the onset and increases the intensity of the distortions. Using overlays can be inappropriate or cumbersome, especially when writing. Instead, colored paper can be used for classroom and homework assignments, for tests, and for taking notes. Which are the best paper colors for that purpose? Beige, yellow, goldenrod, pink, blue, and green have been effective in reducing distortions and increasing contrast and readability for those with SSS. Often a person's most effective paper color will be similar to his or her best overlay color. If you want a universal color to use, try gray, beige, or recycled paper.

Other Modifications

Other things can be done to help students with SSS. Reading materials should be placed directly in front of readers who have SSS problems. All readers with SSS should have their own books. Trying to share materials with other readers can create more problems.

Students with SSS tend not to respond as well to overhead projectors, because of the intense lighting, and even chalkboards can cause them problems. Sometimes, using colored chalk can make reading a little easier. School systems should be made aware of the potential problems students with SSS face when material is presented with overhead projectors or on chalkboards. One thing that has been helpful is having another student—one who does not have SSS—copy the material from the chalkboard or overhead projector so the student with SSS will then be able to read it under better conditions. Whenever possible, the information should be copied onto colored paper.

Some schools are using high-gloss chalkboards in beige or gray rather than white. The new colors make it a lot easier on the eyes.

Colored highlighters, usually found in yellow, pink, or other pastels, can help students read what otherwise might be unreadable or difficult. They especially can help students perform precise academic activities such as keeping numbers in columns, making mathematical computations, or highlighting important information.

Support Services

Because of the significant changes resulting from treatment for SSS, as well as the impact SSS has previously had on the individual, support services can be very helpful. Which support services? Spending time with psychologists, guidance counselors, remediation specialists, and the like, can be invaluable in helping the individual who has SSS deal with the changes he or she is experiencing. Of course, those professionals should be thoroughly familiar with SSS and its impact!

11.

The Future

There are people who have yearned to be academically successful but who have been frustrated for a long time. They have needed to spend so much time completing schoolwork that they haven't had the opportunity to participate in extra-curricular activities. They have forfeited social life, friendships, and recreational activities just to survive in the classroom.

Treatment for SSS provides an alternative for many children and adults who have centered their lives around academics. It offers encouragement and hope for those with reading problems that are perceptually based. The ability to diagnose SSS lets individuals know that they are not personally responsible for poor performance in school. It allows individuals to re-examine the demands being placed on them and their inability to live up to those expectations. SSS provides an explanation for their lack of success, and a simple treatment can produce change so that instead of feeling self-defeat and humiliation, they can look forward to a much brighter future. But despite all the good that has come from the development of SSS treatment techniques, there is much work yet to be done.

NEED FOR RESEARCH

Because the concept of SSS is so new, a lot of research needs to be done over a long period of time by respected educational institutions around the world. There is a great need for outside research to supplement and validate the work being done by Irlen Institute professionals.

Many people are still trying to understand why the Irlen process works. Some of the research, therefore, needs to focus on that important question. There's always more acceptance of a technique when one understands the reasons behind its effectiveness. Unfortunately, the reason for the success of the technique is not clearly understood, yet. And there are certain questions that might never be answered. But there are many things out there that we keep using without being able to explain. For instance, aspirin. Over time, if something continues to work, we eventually just accept it.

SSS IN EDUCATION

If diagnosis and treatment for SSS becomes more recognized and accepted because of its educational and financial benefits, then educators will have more of an open mind as to its appropriate place in their system. All children should be assessed for the presence or absence of SSS at several times during their educational careers. After all, the earlier that experts are able to identify and remediate the problem, the more beneficial it would be for the student. And of course, the more productive and cost-effective it would be for the educational system!

How will SSS testing help the system? Education has been putting a lot of money and energy into too many areas that cannot be corrected at this time. For some children, problems with reading and learning are very severe and require a lot of school resources. If experts can effectively treat SSS, getting rid of that problem, then children with SSS will no longer require as much money, energy, or staff resources. Those resources can then go to other children with other problems. Right now, there are waiting lists for children to get support services. So it would become an overall cost savings for school districts, as well as a benefit to other children who otherwise might not be able to get the help they need.

Holding Things Back

Even when a child gets tested for SSS and colored filters correct the problem, the process is often undermined in the classroom. Comments are being made by professionals who are not convinced of the technique's validity. They might say to the child, "I don't understand why you're wearing those glasses; you don't really need to wear them. You would be able to do your work if you just tried harder. So why do you really think you need them?" It's important that there be a reasonable level of acceptance and support for the process so that the child can at least continue to use the filters in the classroom.

I've seen children in junior high and in high school who have been stopped from wearing the filters because the filters, they are told, are just sunglasses. They're not allowed to wear sunglasses. The same thing holds true for caps and visors. Students are not allowed to wear them in the educational system, even though it would be a very quick, easy, and efficient way to reduce strain and fatigue from fluorescent lighting.

Standardized Testing

Reading difficulties are basically defined by our standardized reading tests, which look only at very specific problems. SSS is concerned with totally different components
of reading: ease and efficiency. There are no standardized
tests that measure or even recognize a person's ease and
efficiency of reading, so it's hard to evaluate changes in
those areas.

It has become evident that there are many dimensions
to learning difficulties. Some have not been previously
researched, but their effects are so profuse that they affect
many areas of performance. Sadly, they too are not detected by the tests currently used to identify and define
learning problems. SSS is not the only area being ignored.
Many more pieces of the puzzle remain to be identified.

Scotopic Sensitivity Syndrome affects how the sufferer perceives the world. But no standardized test asks:
"What does the page look like when you try to read?" No
standardized test, nor any standard treatment method,
has been developed to deal with this answer: "The letters
blend, wave, or float." Or with this one: "The background
is annoying or changing."

Yet those and other distorting effects are, to a greater
or lesser extent, affecting many readers. In addition, the
lighting in classrooms and workplaces, and even high-gloss
pages and the contrast between black and white, can
make reading and sustained attention still more difficult.

Deficiencies in the System

This book aims to educate the public about SSS and
encourage fellow professionals and educators to investi-
gate, from a clearly objective perspective, the actual process of learning. Try to look beyond the constraints of
present-day beliefs regarding the nature of reading diffi-

culties and beyond the current methods for remediating those difficulties.

It should be painfully clear that experts do not have all the answers. With some children who cannot learn or are unable to perform, it's not because they don't want to, but because we professionals have not yet been able to detect the specific reasons for their learning problems.

How often have you seen a child who *wanted* to feel stupid, who was unwilling to try, who purposely chose to spend the largest part of childhood being unsuccessful? Not often! More often, when you come across a child labeled as unmotivated, you'll find a child who has been *unable* to perform. Unfortunately, the limits of the educational system in diagnosing problems have led to inappropriate and damaging labels. What's the best way to diagnose? Ask those who are having the trouble! Amazingly, those individuals, when asked appropriate questions, provide tremendous insight into the cause and nature of their difficulties.

The ability of our educational system to help a greater number of students depends upon its correctly diagnosing their problems. That can be enhanced by incorporating clinical interviews and observations into the diagnostic testing process. The medical profession uses the reporting of symptoms and the observation of behavior as preliminary and essential aspects of correct diagnosis. Shouldn't education do the same? The educational community has become fixated on the need to administer standardized tests in trying to detect problems. Unfortunately, that has resulted in an abandonment of the essential aspects of self-reporting and observation. How many more pieces of the puzzle are waiting to be discovered? How many more children could be helped? Children are our most valuable resource. No child should suffer needlessly if we can find the answers.

SSS IN THE ENVIRONMENT

A greater sensitivity to environmental conditions can aid perceptual ease and comfort. Right now, school and work-place environments are geared for the non-scotopic person. That's why everything is under bright or fluorescent lighting. Black print on white pages is considered the best contrast for reading, even though it's far from best for many people with SSS; also, high gloss, another problem maker, is in, be it in textbooks or on chalkboards. Normally, we don't think about color, glare, comfort, or the type or intensity of lighting. Therefore, there are easy modifications that can be made for a population that has been ignored up to now. If those areas were changed, it would make very little difference to the non-scotopic population but would be a great help to those who are scotopic.

IN SUMMARY

Well, there you have it. A detailed discussion of Scotopic Sensitivity Syndrome, designed to educate, stimulate, challenge, and encourage. For those of you who will directly benefit from what you've read, who will go through the process and obtain colored overlays or filters, enjoy the new world that reading by the colors can provide!

Clinics: Where to Turn for Help

I rlen Institute headquarters is at 5380 Village Road, Long Beach, CA 90808. Its telephone number is (213) 496-2550. The institute offers full SSS screening and treatment. Such services are also offered at other clinics. A listing of all such clinics and many of their directors soon follows. But first, a word on screeners.

Besides the clinics, there are hundreds of individuals—mostly educators and psychologists—highly qualified to offer professional screening for Scotopic Sensitivity Syndrome. Unfortunately, they are not equipped to select or create the proper filters for the SSS sufferer. But because they are so much more numerous than clinics, it might be more convenient for a person to be screened for SSS by just such a professional and then, if the results of the screening warrant it, to head for a clinic for SSS treatment. For the names and phone numbers of SSS screeners near you, contact the SSS clinic nearest you.

In addition, ten countries that lack SSS clinics contain qualified SSS screeners: Belgium, Canada, Germany, Israel,

187

Japan, Jordan, Pakistan, Switzerland, New Zealand, and the U.S.S.R. If you live in any of those countries and wish to be screened, Irlen Institute headquarters can tell you how to contact the screener nearest you.

UNITED STATES CLINICS

Alaska
Barb Robek
Box 110214 South Station
Anchorage, AK 99511
(907) 345–0894

California
Larry & Diana Beutler
622 13th Street
Modesto, CA 95354
(209) 577–0880

Center for Perceptual Care
1551 East Cypress
Suite E
Redding, CA 96002
(916) 223–4586

Colorado
Jetta Associates Inc.
5290 East Yale Circle
#204
Denver, CO 80222
(303) 757–4930

Florida
Dr. Sharon Smisek
3920 N.E. 27th Avenue
Lighthouse Point, FL 33064
(305) 782–0496

Dr. Van W. Tilford
2390 Old US 441
Suite 3
Mount Dora, FL 32757
(904) 383–1911

Hawaii
Lynn Miller
3316 Woodlawn Drive
Honolulu, HI 96822
(808) 988–3060

Illinois
Irlen Clinic
500 Davis Street
Suite 503
Evanston, IL 60201
(708) 475–3700

Kansas
Midstates Associates
3301 Clinton Parkway Court
Suite 1
Lawrence, KS 66047
(913) 749–3838

Louisiana
Dr. Lee D. Stokes
P.O. Box 767
Covington, LA 70434
(504) 893–7227

Massachusetts
Irlen Clinic
One Kendall Square
Building 700
Cambridge, MA 92139
(617) 621-0830

Michigan
Barbara David
4938 Coventry
Royal Oak, MI 48073
(313) 280-2719

Minnesota
Marilyn Nathenson
8549 Irwin Road
#234
Minneapolis, MN 55437
(612) 831-5803

Nevada
Marilyn Nathenson
4220 Gannet Circle
#298
Las Vegas, NV 89103
(702) 251-1117

New York
Irlen Clinic
1776 Broadway
Suite 1610
New York, NY 10019
(212) 397-9620

North Carolina
Jo Adair Swan
3309 Watauga Drive
Greensboro, NC 27410
(919) 292-2131

Oklahoma
Irlen Clinic
#4 Ardmore Mall
Ardmore, OK 73401
(405) 226-8477

Pennsylvania
Susan Smith
4238 Prestwick Drive
Erie, PA 16506
(814) 833-2988

Texas
Zuccone & Associates
6065 Hillcroft
Suite 607
Houston, TX 77081
(713) 771-3108

OTHER CLINICS

Australia
Irlen Clinic
6 The Highway
P.O. Box 524
Mount Waverley, Victoria
3149
3-807-7822

Irlen Diagnostic Clinic for
Reading & Perceptual
Disorders
84 Canberra Avenue
P.O. Box 3018
Manuka, Australian Capital
Territory 2603
6-295-1319

Irlen Clinic
P.O. Box 290
Palmerston, Northern
    Territory 0830
89–272–244

Dr. Gregory L. Robinson
Special Education Centre
University of Newcastle
Rankin Drive
P.O. Box 84
Waratah, New South Wales
    2298
49–216–277

Irlen Clinic
P.O. Box 240
Applecross 6153
Western Australia
9–330–4922

Dr. Paul R. Whiting
Evelyn McCloughan
    Children's Centre
University of Sydney
A22 Carillon Avenue
Newtown 2006
New South Wales
2–516–4389

Irlen Diagnostic Clinic—
    N. Qld.
353 Stanley Street
North Ward Townsville
Queensland 4810
77–713–572

Irlen Diagnostic Clinic
Suite 4
512 Swift Street
Albury, New South Wales
    2640
60–216–151

Edcare Professional Services
Commonwealth Bank Building
Barclay Street
St. Kilda, Victoria 3182
3–537–2661

Hamilton Education Centre
Thompson Street
Hamilton, Victoria 3300
55–723–811

Irlen Diagnostic Clinic
P.O. Box 1117
Port Macquarie, New South
    Wales 2444
65–841–272

Irlen Diagnostic Clinic
P.O. Box 966
Unley, South Australia 5063
8–373–3590

Irlen Clinic
22 Knox Street
P.O. Box 522
Dalby, Queensland 4405
76–622–065

New England Irlen Clinic
P.O. Box 1330
Armidale, New South Wales
2350
67–729–686

Irlen Diagnostic Clinic
P.O. Box 696
Maroochydore, Queensland
4558
74–431–611

Irlen Diagnostic Clinic & Kip
McGrath Education Centre
77 Postle Street
Coopers Plains
Brisbane, Queensland 4108
7–277–6257

Irlen Diagnostic Clinic—
M.W. NSW
79 Macquarie Street
P.O. Box 1403
Dubbo, New South Wales 2830
68–843–088

Hong Kong
Dr. Irene G. Allinson
Chinese University of
Hong Kong
Residence 15/5B
Shatin, N.T.
692–0456

Ireland
Reading Clinic
Passage West
Co. Cork
Republic of Ireland
84–1437

Marita McGeady
King's Hospital
Palmerstown, Dublin 20
Republic of Ireland
26–3058

Netherlands
Drs. Dirk J. Graaff
Venushof 13
Maarn 3951 EN
31–3432–2843

United Kingdom
North-West Irlen Centre
Beacon Lodge
Macclesfield Road
Nether Alderley, Macclesfield
Cheshire SK10 4UB
England
625–583841

Irlen Centre
9 Orme Court
London W24RL
England
71–229–8810

Yorkshire Irlen Centre
Woodhouse Grove School
Apperley Bridge
Bradford BD10 0NR
England
532–509150

Somerset & Avon Irlen Centre
107 Bath Road
Bridgwater
Somerset
England
278–426695

Northern Ireland Irlen Centre
9 Carol Hill Drive
Holywood Road
Belfast 4
Northern Ireland
232–653841

South Wales Irlen Centre
151 Derwen Fawr Road
Swansea
West Glamorgan SA2 8ED
Wales
792–206312

North Wales & Shropshire
    Irlen Centre
Meadow House
75 Barnston Road
Heswall
Wirral L60 1UE
Wales
51–342–5789

West Country Irlen Centre
123 High Street, Chard
South Somerset TA201QT
England
46–06–5555

East Anglia Irlen Centre
Old School House, West Stow
Bury St. Edmunds
Suffolk IP28 6EX
England
284–728623

Index

Abstract reasoning, 81
Aphasia, developmental, 80
Attention, sustained, lack of, 31, 48
Attention deficit disorder, 31, 71, 85
Attention span, 31, 81, 86

Background accommodation, inadequate, 31, 33–37
Behavior problems, 111–112, 175
Blurry effect, 45
Brain deficit, 57, 98
Brain injury, 80

California State University–Long Beach, 16
Choral reading, 75
Colored filters. See Filters.
Colored lenses. See Filters.

Colored overlays. See Overlays.
Comprehension, reading, 61, 63, 70, 88
Concentration, 81
Contrast, high, 33

Depth perception, 31, 55, 116–117, 145
Diagnosing SSS, 4, 127–145
Distortions, 5, 60–61, 76
Dyscalculia, 31
Dyslexia, 6, 7, 31, 50, 80, 83, 85, 95–109, 156
  brain and, 98
  causes of, 97–98
  definition, 96
  impact of, 95
  problems from, 97
  SSS and, 98–109

Education for All
    Handicapped Children
    Act of 1975, 79–80
Educational intervention, 4
Energy level, 31
Eye strain, 69

Fatigue, 48, 68, 138
Fernald method, 75
Filters, 24, 57, 74, 76, 101,
    122, 123, 145, 155–159,
    163–164, 167, 171, 173,
    174, 175
Fluorescent lighting, 32, 55,
    71–72, 176–177, 183,
    186
Folayan, Ayofemi, 32

Gels. See Overlays.
Gross motor activities, 31,
    84–85, 88

Halo effect, 38
Handwriting, 31, 88, 121
Headaches, 32, 37, 48, 51,
    68–69
Hemingway, Margaux, 95

Incandescent lighting, 176
Inefficient reading, 49, 51
Irlen Institute, 27, 50, 109,
    187
Irradiation, 34

Jordan, Dale, 50

Language experience
    approach, 75
Learning disabilities, 7, 14,
    26, 50, 79–94, 96, 97
    assessing, 85–88

brain and, 83
causes, 82–83
definition, 79–80
hereditary factor in, 83
magnitude, 80–81
nickname, 79
problems from, 81–82
SSS and, 87–92
treatment, 92–94
types of, 83–85
Lenses. See Filters.
Light, wavelengths, 1, 57
Light sensitivity, 31, 32–33
Linguistic method, 75

Motivation, 31, 113–114
Motor skills. See Gross
    motor activities.

Nausea, 51, 68, 69

Orton, Samuel, 98
Orton Dyslexia Society, 98,
    108, 109
Orton–Guillingham method,
    75
Overlap effect, 41
Overlays, 22–23, 74, 129,
    139–145, 171

Paired reading method, 76
Peer pressure, 174–175
Perceptual dysfunction, 1, 7,
    29, 65, 75
Phonetics, 74, 75
Photospectrometer, 24, 159
Print resolution, poor, 31,
    37–43
Psychological testing, 15
Public Law 94–142. See
    Education for All

Handicapped Children Act of 1975.

"Reading by the Colors," 27
Reading comprehension, 61, 63, 70, 88
Recorded book, 76
Resolution, print. *See* Print resolution.
Rivers effect, 40
"Rose Coloured Glasses," 26
Rotation table, 10

Scotopic Sensitivity Syndrome
  attitude problems from, 112–113
  behavior problems from, 111–112
  brain and, 57
  depth perception and, 116–117
  dyslexia and, 98–109
  effects of, 2–3, 30–31
  filters and, 155–159, 163–164
  heredity and, 57–58
  learning disabilities and, 87–94
  magnitude of, 2
  math and, 120–121
  music and, 119–120
  name, 1, 29
  overlays and, 139–142
  reading and, 59–77
  screening and, 127–145
  self-esteem and, 115–116
  sports and, 117–118
  writing and, 121–125

Scotopic vision, 29
Seesaw effect, 46
Self-esteem, 2, 82, 97, 115–116
Sensory-motor integration therapy, 19, 56
Shaky effect, 44
60 Minutes, 26–27, 108, 109
60 Minutes Australia, 25–26
Span of recognition, restricted, 31, 43, 47
Spectral modification, 29, 155–156
Spectrum, 29, 57
SSS. *See* Scotopic Sensitivity Syndrome.
Standardized tests, 9, 14–15, 17, 72–74, 76–77, 88, 131, 184
Sustained attention, lack of, 31, 48
Swirl effect, 42
Sydney University, 26

Teacher evaluations, 9, 15
Tracking, 39, 56, 134
Tunnel reading, 47

Vision therapy, 10, 19, 22, 56

Washout effect, 36
Whiting, Dr. Paul, 26
Whole-word approach, 75
World Federation of Neurology, 96